LIVING IN STYLE
MALLORCA

Edited by Christine von Auersperg
Texts by Tiny von Wedel

teNeues

Contents

Introduction	4
Refugi a Orient	10
Son Bielo	18
Torre del Mar	28
Son Coll	34
Castell de Bendinat	44
Casa Son Vida	48
Palacio Feliu	58
Ca'n Montesión	66
Oratorio de Sant Feliu	74
Palacio blanco-negro	82
Parlament Apartment	90
Ca'n Blau	98
Finca sa Pedra	106
Son Silvestre	114
Grimalt Charming	120
Natural Conclusion	124
Casa Neuendorf	130
Son Almendros	138
La Ruina	148
Son Llodra	156
Son Moix	164
Sa Canova	174
Es Puig	182
Ses Eres III	190
Sa Fortaleza	200
Ca'n Suau Vell	208
Casa Bauzà	214
Index	222
Biographies	223
Credits & Imprint	224

Introduction

The largest island in the Balearic archipelago, Majorca is practically a small country surrounded by the sea. Thanks to its cosmopolitan capital, Palma, and a checkered history of Roman conquests, Moorish occupation and pirates, the island forms the ideal backdrop for the diverse architectural and interior design styles of the homes belonging to Majorca's international community. The landscape is as colorful as the island's history, featuring bougainvillea, pine trees, almond and olive groves, rugged mountain chains and shorelines that seem to go on forever. Stylish sanctuaries for every taste can be found here, from Mediterranean country homes and classic urban mansions to purist designer homes. They all bask in the sublime light that bathes the "isla de la luz" (Island of Light).

Majorca is a land of four climates and four landscapes. Rarely does nature bless a single island with such great diversity—lush vegetation, old-growth forests, remote valleys, craggy rock formations and endless, white beaches. The island's Mediterranean climate and easy-going lifestyle also shape its typically Mediterranean architecture. Many homes are built from traditional marès sandstone, and their walls scatter the sunlight into myriad shades of ever-changing color. Surrounded by red earth and vibrant green Mediterranean flora, Majorca stages a magnificent color show right in the middle of the azure sea.

The members of Majorca's international community invite the reader into their homes for a rare glimpse of rural estates, minimalist urban pieds-à-terre, magnificent townhouses and the classic mansions of long-established Spanish families. The architectural styles and interior design appear as varied as their natural surroundings. At times, the contemporary architecture offers an attractive counterpoint to nature's primordial panoramas, while the Mediterranean architecture is interpreted in exciting ways to create new modern classics. In the houses, art objects and veritable treasures brought home from all over the world share space with historic architectural features, some of which go all the way back to the 12th century, as though the island's current residents had taken up Majorca's long tradition of piracy. 21st-century art, combined with classic design and luxurious comfort lend a unique atmosphere to the interiors, whose individuality reflects the personalities of the owners.

Some of the homes are their owners' principle residences, while others are seasonal getaways. They all feature a pleasing mix of Mediterranean traditional and international style, with great attention to detail and a sense of the island's spirit. From understated luxury to classic purism, remote rural oases to light-filled apartments in the island's vibrant metropolis, this book showcases Mediterranean living at its best!

Tiny von Wedel

Einleitung

Als größte der Balearischen Inseln ist Mallorca fast schon ein kleines Land im Meer. Mit ihrer kosmopolitischen Metropole Palma und einer bewegten Geschichte mit Römern, Mauren und Piraten bietet die Insel die ideale Leinwand für die verschiedenen individuellen Baustile und Interieurs der internationalen Cognoscenti, die hier ihre Häuser haben. So vielschichtig wie die Geschichte sind auch die Landschaften, geprägt von Bougainvilleen, Pinien, Mandel- und Olivenbäumen, schroffen Bergketten und endlosen Küstenstreifen. Von mediterranen Landhäusern über klassische Stadtpaläste bis hin zu puristischen Designhäusern findet man hier stilvolle Rückzugsorte unterschiedlicher Couleur. Doch alle sind sie durchflutet von dem unvergleichlichen Licht der „isla de la luz", der „Insel des Lichts".

Mallorca ist eine Vier-Wetter- und Vier-Landschaften-Insel. Selten findet man eine so große Vielfalt der Natur – üppige Vegetation, alter Baumbestand, einsame Täler, zerklüftete Felsformationen und endlose, weiße Strände – auf einem Eiland vereint. Das mediterrane Klima und der südländische Lebensstil prägen auch die typisch mediterrane Architektur und traditionelle Bauweise aus Marès-Stein, auf dessen Mauern sich das Sonnenlicht in immer neuen Farbnuancen bricht. Umgeben von der roten Erde des Landes und dem kräftigen Grün der Mittelmeerflora entsteht so ein prachtvolles Farbenspiel inmitten des azurblauen Wassers.

Die internationale Inselgemeinschaft hat für dieses Buch ihre Türen geöffnet und gewährt Einblicke in ländliche Anwesen, minimalistisch-urbane Pieds-à-terre, herrschaftliche Stadthäuser und klassische Herrenhäuser alter spanischer Familien. So vielseitig wie die Umgebung sind auch die Bau- und Einrichtungsstile. Die zeitgenössische Architektur bildet oft einen attraktiven Kontrast zu den ursprünglichen Naturpanoramen, die Mittelmeerarchitektur wird auf modern-klassische Art spannend neu interpretiert. Und als wäre die lange Piratentradition Mallorcas auf die neuen Inselbewohner übergegangen, finden sich auch in den Häusern Beute- und Kunstgegenstände aus aller Welt, Seite an Seite mit historischen Bauelementen, die zum Teil bis in das 12. Jahrhundert zurückreichen. Mit Kunst aus dem 21. Jahrhundert, Designklassikern und State-of-the-Art Komfort sind hier Interieurs entstanden, die eine einzigartige Atmosphäre erzeugen und in ihrer Individualität die Persönlichkeiten ihrer Besitzer widerspiegeln.

Die Häuser dienen zum Teil als Hauptwohnsitze, zum Teil nur als saisonal genutzte Refugien, sind aber allesamt Beispiele für eine gelungene Mischung aus mediterraner Tradition und internationalen Stilelementen, mit viel Gespür für Details und den Geist des Ortes. Ob zurückgezogener Luxus oder repräsentativer Purismus, abgelegene Landoase oder lichtdurchflutete Stadtwohnung in einer der pulsierendsten Inselmetropolen des Mittelmeeres: Mediterranean at its best!

Tiny von Wedel

Introducción

Mallorca, la mayor de las islas Baleares, es casi un país entero rodeado por el mar. Con su cosmopolita capital, Palma, y con una historia por la que han pasado romanos, moros y piratas, la isla ofrece el marco ideal para los distintos estilos arquitectónicos y de interiorismo de la comunidad internacional que ha hecho de ella su hogar. Y tan multifacético como su historia es el paisaje de Mallorca, marcado por las buganvillas, los pinos, los almendros y los olivos, por escarpadas montañas e interminables tramos costeros. Villas mediterráneas, palacetes urbanos, puristas viviendas de diseño... En Mallorca es posible encontrar el reposo en residencias de todo tamaño y condición, pero todas tienen algo en común: la incomparable claridad que baña la «isla de la luz».

Mallorca es un lugar de estaciones y paisajes cambiantes. Resulta difícil creer que en una misma isla pueda darse semejante diversidad natural: lustrosa vegetación, bosques primigenios, valles solitarios, escarpadas formaciones rocosas, extensas playas de arena blanca... El clima y el estilo de vida mediterráneo están también muy presentes en la arquitectura y las técnicas tradicionales de construcción con piedra de marès, que crea muros sobre los que la luz solar se descompone en matices siempre cambiantes. Y así, rodeado por el tono rojizo de la arcilla local y por el verde intenso de la flora mediterránea, asoma toda una gama de colores de entre el azul del mar.

La comunidad internacional de la isla ha querido abrir sus puertas a los lectores de este libro, y nos ha permitido asomarnos a residencias rurales, minimalistas *pieds-à-terre* urbanos, señoriales casas de ciudad y villas clásicas de familias españolas. La enorme variedad paisajística de la isla tiene reflejo en los múltiples estilos arquitectónicos y de diseño de interiores. La arquitectura contemporánea contrasta a menudo de manera muy atractiva con los parajes naturales en los que se inscribe, y el tradicional estilo mediterráneo es objeto de una interesante reinterpretación a un tiempo clásica y moderna. Y además, como si la larga tradición de piratería en Mallorca hubiese calado en los nuevos habitantes de la isla, en estas casas pueden encontrarse auténticos tesoros y objetos de arte procedentes de todo el mundo, a menudo junto a elementos arquitectónicos históricos que en algunos casos se remontan hasta el siglo XII. De la combinación de arte del siglo XXI, clásicos del diseño y confort superlativo resultan unos interiores de ambientación única, cuya individualidad refleja la personalidad de sus distintos propietarios.

Algunas de estas casas son residencias principales, otras sirven como refugio de temporada, pero todas son ejemplo de una lograda conjunción de tradición mediterránea y elementos internacionales en la que brilla la atención al detalle y el respeto por el espíritu del lugar. Ya se trate de lujo retraído o de exuberante purismo, del más recóndito remanso de paz o de una vivienda urbana bañada por la luz en el bullicio de la metrópoli isleña: a lo largo de las páginas siguientes encontraremos algunas de las mejores residencias de toda Mallorca.

Tiny von Wedel

Refugi a Orient

Orient

Situated in the heart of the Tramuntana Mountains, surrounded by centuries-old oak trees, the house radiates fresh tranquility and comfortable harmony with its simple design and monochrome color scheme. In building and furnishing the home, the all-female team of architects with Sagristà Simó Arquitectes emphasized sustainability and the use of natural materials. The untreated wood surfaces and natural hues create a functional, homey atmosphere, while a special ecological and holistic ventilation system maintains just the right temperature all year round. The floor is made of locally harvested pine and provides a charming contrast to the concrete ceiling beams in the airy, light-filled rooms. A fenestrated facade that forms the walls combines the indoor and outdoor spaces to create a harmonious whole.

Das Haus im Herzen des Tramuntana-Gebirges, inmitten jahrhundertealter Eichenbäume, strahlt in seiner Schlichtheit und monochromen Farbgebung eine frische Ruhe und warme Harmonie aus. Beim Bau und bei der Einrichtung legten die Architektinnen von Sagristà Simó Arquitectes großen Wert auf Nachhaltigkeit und die Verwendung von Naturmaterialien. Die unbehandelten Holzoberflächen und Naturtöne schaffen eine funktionelle, behagliche Atmosphäre, und ein spezielles ökologisch-ganzheitliches Belüftungssystem sorgt das ganze Jahr über für optimale Temperaturen. Der Boden ist aus Pinienholz der Region gefertigt und bildet einen reizvollen Kontrast zu den Beton-Deckenbalken in den luftigen, lichtdurchfluteten Räumen. Durch die wandfüllenden Fensterfronten verbinden sich Innen- und Außenbereiche zu einem harmonischen Ganzen.

Rodeada de encinas centenarias en pleno corazón de la Serra de Tramuntana, la casa irradia serenidad y armonía en su sencillez y monotonía cromática. Tanto en la construcción como en el diseño de interiores, las arquitectas de Sagristà Simó Arquitectes quisieron enfatizar la sostenibilidad y el uso de materiales naturales. Las superficies de madera sin tratar y los colores naturales generan un ambiente confortable y funcional, mientras que un sistema especial de ventilación integral ecológico permite disfrutar de una temperatura ideal durante todo el año. El suelo es de madera de pino local y ofrece un agradable contraste con las vigas de hormigón de las luminosas y amplias habitaciones. Los ventanales ocupan toda la pared y comunican las zonas interiores y exteriores para construir un armónico conjunto.

Refugi a Orient 15

Son Bielo

Serra de Tramuntana

Located in the Serra de Tramuntana mountains in the northern part of the island, this 13th-century former bishop's residence was brought back to life after many years of neglect by the architect Antonio Obrador. The historic mansion, which had long remained uninhabited, covers a vast 8,600 square feet of living space, including a private chapel. The architect's fine instinct for uncovering the essence of old buildings helped create a cozy sanctuary with a magical ambience. The owner-decorated rooms radiate casual elegance, and the interior design is a harmonious blend of contemporary art and antiques that both preserves and transforms tradition.

Der ehemalige Bischofssitz aus dem 13. Jahrhundert liegt inmitten der Bergkette Serra de Tramuntana im Norden der Insel und wurde vom Architekten Antonio Obrador aus seinem Dornröschenschlaf zu neuem Leben erweckt. Das viele Jahre unbewohnte Herrenhaus mit langer Geschichte erstreckt sich über weitläufige 800 Quadratmeter Wohnfläche mitsamt eigener Hauskapelle. Mit feinem Gespür für die Seele historischer Bauten wurde hier ein Refugium mit magischer Atmosphäre und familiärem Charakter geschaffen. Die von den Eigentümern gestalteten Räume strahlen eine informelle Lässigkeit und Eleganz aus. Die Einrichtung ist eine harmonische Mischung aus zeitgenössischer Kunst und Antiquitäten, die Tradition gleichzeitig fortführt und erneuert.

La antigua residencia episcopal del siglo XIII se encuentra al norte de la isla, en plena Serra de Tramuntana, y ha sido recuperada de su letargo por el arquitecto Antonio Obrador. La histórica casa señorial, vacía durante muchos años, dispone de unos espaciosos 800 metros cuadrados y cuenta con una capilla propia. Se ha creado aquí un verdadero refugio de atmósfera embrujadora y de carácter familiar, respetando en todo momento el alma histórica del edificio. Las habitaciones, diseñadas por los propietarios, destilan elegancia informal, fruto de una armoniosa combinación de arte contemporáneo y antigüedades con la que se prolonga y renueva simultáneamente la tradición.

An enormous painting by Ramon Canet, a prominent Majorcan artist, hangs next to artfully-arranged 18th-century chairs and the portrait of one of the owner's ancestors, who once held the office of a bishop. Together, these treasures form a harmonious atmosphere, in which the owner's Labradors make themselves right at home.

Ein großformatiges Gemälde des bedeutenden mallorquinischen Künstlers Ramon Canet hängt neben gefassten Stühlen aus dem 18. Jahrhundert und dem Porträt eines Urahnen des Hausherrn, der ebenfalls ein Bischofsamt bekleidete. Das harmonische Gesamtbild wird nur noch von den Hauslabradoren abgerundet.

Un cuadro de gran formato del destacado artista mallorquín Ramon Canet, expuesto junto a sillas del siglo XVIII y el retrato de un antepasado del propietario, investido también de la dignidad episcopal. Todos estos tesoros conforman un todo armónico por el que transitan constantemente los dos labradores de la residencia.

Son Bielo

Torre del Mar

Lluc Alcari

The historic 15th-century building and adjacent tower are situated on Majorca's picturesque northwestern coast. Uscha Behrends-Wagner, its owner, lovingly restored and furnished the house over a period of two years. The result is a Mediterranean sanctuary with Bohemian charm, steeped in history. The entrance leads through a traditional Majorcan arched gate into a beautifully-landscaped patio, the perfect setting for selected antiques, statues and stone benches. The adjacent sprawling building and the tower contain the living area, a studio and three bedrooms whose indigenous accents and warm colors create different moods. The rooftop terrace, with its panoramic ocean view, is a good place to enjoy a typical Mediterranean siesta in the shade of a pergola.

Das antike Gebäude mit eindrucksvollem Turm aus dem 15. Jahrhundert liegt an Mallorcas malerischer Nordwestküste. Seine Besitzerin, Uscha Behrends-Wagner, hat es über zwei Jahre liebevoll restauriert und eingerichtet. Das Ergebnis: ein mediterraner Rückzugsort mit Bohemien-Charme und Geschichte. Der Eingang führt durch einen landestypischen Torbogen in einen wunderschön bewachsenen Patio, der szenisch mit ausgesuchten Antiquitäten, Statuen und Steinbänken dekoriert ist. Auf das daran angrenzende verwinkelte Hauptgebäude und den Turm verteilen sich Wohnraum, Studio und drei Schlafzimmer, die mit ethnischen Elementen und warmen Farben ausgestattet sind und unterschiedliche Stimmungen wiedergeben. Die Dachterrasse mit Panorama-Meerblick bietet unter einer schattigen Pergola einen weiteren typisch mediterranen Ort der Entspannung.

El antiguo edificio y su impresionante torreón se alzan desde el siglo XV en la pintoresca costa noroeste de Mallorca, y han sido cuidadosamente restaurados y acondicionados a lo largo de dos años por su propietaria Uscha Behrends-Wagner. El resultado es un refugio mediterráneo con mucha historia y un extraordinario encanto bohemio. El portal típico de la isla abre paso a un maravilloso patio ajardinado y decorado con selectas antigüedades, estatuas y bancos de piedra. Tras este se encuentran el edificio principal y la torre, en cuyo interior hallamos un salón con un estudio y tres dormitorios cuya decoración con elementos étnicos y colores cálidos evoca sensaciones y estados de ánimo muy diferenciados. En la azotea, a la sombra de la pérgola, las amplias vistas al mar completan un espacio típicamente mediterráneo en el que olvidar toda preocupación.

Torre del Mar 33

Son Coll

Port d'es Canonge

The Son Coll country estate was once an olive mill and has a manor house that dates back to the 15th century. In its early days, the finca supplied fruit and vegetables to the entire village, and the locals still refer to this country estate as the "supply finca." The vast, terraced grounds extend all the way to the sea. The owners took great care in renovating the house and restored all the historic sections to their original glory, creating an atmosphere where time seems to stand still. They preserved the original mill, along with the rooms that were used for pressing and refining the olive oil. The interior design reflects the building's classic style, with exquisite fabrics and antiques that lend the rooms a quiet, dignified elegance. Many pieces of furniture are antiques that came with the house when the new owner's family moved in.

Das Landgut Son Coll ist eine ehemalige Olivenmühle mit dazugehörigem Herrenhaus aus dem 15. Jahrhundert. Die Finca versorgte damals das gesamte Dorf mit Obst und Gemüse und wird daher im Ort immer noch „die Versorgerfinca" genannt. Das weitläufige Gelände zieht sich terassenförmig bis hinunter ans Meer. Das Haus wurde behutsam renoviert, alle historischen Gebäudeteile hat man originalgetreu restauriert – so entstand eine Atmosphäre, in der die Zeit stehen geblieben zu sein scheint. Die ursprüngliche Ölmühle wurde ebenso erhalten wie die dazugehörigen Räume zur Pressung und weiteren Verarbeitung des Olivenöls. Bei der Einrichtung der Räume hat man den klassischen Stil des Hauses aufgenommen; die edlen Stoffe und Antiquitäten verleihen dem Ambiente eine gediegene, unaufgeregte Eleganz. Viele der Möbel sind antike Stücke, die schon im Haus waren, als die neue Besitzerfamilie es übernahm.

La possessió de Son Coll es una antigua almazara del siglo XV de la que se conserva también la mansión señorial. En otra época, la finca surtía de fruta y verdura a toda la aldea, por lo que en la zona se la conoce todavía como «la finca de las provisiones». La extensa propiedad se prolonga en terrazas escalonadas hasta la misma orilla del mar. La casa ha sido cuidadosamente renovada y se ha procurado restaurar las distintas alas respetando el diseño original, con lo que el tiempo parece haberse detenido en su interior. El molino de aceite se ha conservado en su estado original, así como las correspondientes salas para el prensado y elaboración del aceite de oliva. La decoración de las habitaciones ha respetado el estilo clásico del edificio: las nobles telas y las antigüedades aportan una sutil y templada elegancia al ambiente. Muchos de los muebles son auténticas antigüedades que ya estaban en la casa cuando la adquirieron sus actuales propietarios.

The pews and the altar in the small chapel are original pieces that lend a special charm to the sprawling property.

Die Kirchenbänke in der kleinen Kapelle sind ebenso wie der Altar Originalstücke, die dem verwinkelten Anwesen einen besonderen Charme verleihen.

Tanto el altar como las banquetas de la capilla son piezas originales que confieren un encanto especial a la laberíntica propiedad.

Son Coll

Polo practice and games with the estate's own ponies, as well as international tournaments, are held on a polo field surrounded by pine hedges.

Auf dem von Pinienhecken eingezäunten Poloplatz finden außer dem Training und den Spielen mit hauseigenen Poloponys auch internationale Turniere statt.

El campo de polo, delimitado por altos setos, no solo se emplea para los entrenamientos y partidos de los caballos de la propiedad, sino es también escenario de torneos internacionales.

Castell de Bendinat

Bendinat

Located near Palma, Castell de Bendinat was built in the style of a neo-gothic castle in the second half of the 19th century. With its characteristic arched gable windows, the imposing building presides over a lush garden landscape that once formed part of an enormous park with an artificial pond. Sandstone lends a warm hue to the outer facade with its four gabled towers, a color that stands out against the surrounding landscape and turns a deep shade of terra-cotta at dusk. The current owners invested a great deal of time and money into restoring the home, and they were able to largely preserve the magnificent wall paintings, ceilings and decorative features. The house exudes history. In the entrance hall, massive furnishings made of aluminum, combined with the rest of the classic yet modern interior design, create a highly-charged ambience.

In der zweiten Hälfte des 19. Jahrhunderts entstand in der Nähe von Palma dieses schlossähnliche Anwesen im neogotischen Stil. Mit seinen charakteristischen Spitzgiebelfenstern thront es imposant inmitten einer üppigen Gartenlandschaft, die vormals Teil eines riesigen Parks inklusive künstlichem Teich war. Der Sandstein verleiht der Außenfassade mit den vier Giebeltürmen eine warme Färbung, die sich von der umliegenden Landschaft abhebt und in den Abendstunden in ein tiefes Terrakotta übergeht. Die heutigen Eigentümer haben das Gebäude aufwendig restauriert und die prächtigen Wandgemälde, Deckenkonstruktionen und Dekorationselemente dabei größtenteils erhalten können. Das Haus atmet Geschichte. In der Eingangshalle stehen massiv wirkende moderne Einrichtungselemente aus Aluminium, die zusammen mit der übrigen klassisch-modernen Ausstattung ein spannungsgeladenes Ambiente erzeugen.

En la segunda mitad del siglo XIX se construyó en las afueras de Palma este remedo de castillo neogótico. Sus características ventanas ojivales asoman imponentes por encima de un frondoso espacio ajardinado que en tiempos formó parte de un inmenso parque dotado incluso de un lago artificial. La arenisca de la fachada y los cuatro torreones le confieren un color muy cálido que muta hacia tonos rojizos al caer la tarde y le permite destacarse en el paisaje circundante. Los actuales propietarios han restaurado minuciosamente el edificio y han conseguido en buena medida conservar los espléndidos murales, techados y elementos decorativos originales. En toda la casa se respira historia. El recibidor ha incorporado elementos modernos de aluminio que, combinados con la modernidad clásica del resto del equipamiento, crean un ambiente palpitante y muy atractivo.

Castell de Bendinat

A harmonious blend of modern lighting design, classic furniture and high-quality, one-of-a-kind antiques creates an elegantly distinguished ambience in the spacious rooms. The color of the walls generates a warm mood that is emphasized by the parquet floor.

Die harmonische Mischung aus modernem Lichtdesign, klassischem Mobiliar und wertvollen antiken Einzelstücken sorgt in den weitläufigen Räumen für ein elegant-repräsentatives Ambiente. Die durch die Wandfarbe erzeugte warme Stimmung wird vom Parkettboden noch unterstrichen.

La armoniosa combinación del diseño de luces, mobiliario clásico y valiosas antigüedades conforma un espacio elegante y solemne. El entarimado contribuye a subrayar los tonos cálidos de las paredes.

Casa Son Vida

Son Vida

Partially-painted external facades amplify the impact of this building's futuristic architecture. tecArchitecture, a company based in Los Angeles and Switzerland, came up with the space-age design. The architects used the latest structural engineering technologies in creating the building's unusual, innovative use of form and structure. They also paid a great deal of attention to environmentally-friendly building construction, which earned the house a Green Building award. Designer Marcel Wanders came up with the glamorous, high-tech interior design and transformed it into a kind of utopian living space. Casa Son Vida is the first of six progressive design projects being planned by Cosmopolitan Estates Ltd., which will completely redefine Mediterranean architecture and place Majorca right in the center of the international world of elite design.

Die futuristisch anmutende Architektur dieses Hauses wird durch die teilweise bemalten Außenfassaden in ihrer Wirkung noch verstärkt. Für das ultraspacige Design zeichnet sich die in Los Angeles und der Schweiz ansässige Firma tecArchitecture verantwortlich. Sie verwendete für die ungewohnte, innovative Formensprache und Struktur des Gebäudes neueste Konstruktionstechnologien und legte zudem Wert auf eine ökologische Bauweise, für die das Haus bereits als „Green Building" ausgezeichnet wurde. Designer Marcel Wanders entwarf das Glamour-Hightech-Design der Innenräume und verwandelte sie in eine Art utopischen Wohntraum. Casa Son Vida ist das erste von sechs weiteren geplanten progressiven Designprojekten der Cosmopolitan Estates Ltd., die den mediterranen Baustil völlig neu definieren und Mallorca in das Zentrum der internationalen Designelite rücken werden.

La imágenes que decoran la fachada de esta sorprendente residencia no hacen sino resaltar su aire decididamente futurista, obra del despacho de arquitectos tecArchitecture, con sedes en Los Ángeles y Suiza. El insospechado e innovador lenguaje formal empleado y la estructura se valen de las más modernas tecnologías, sin por ello dejar de lado las consideraciones ecológicas: la vivienda ha merecido distinciones por su carácter de «edificio verde». El diseñador Marcel Wanders concibió el interiorismo, glamouroso y high-tech, y transformó los espacios interiores en una asombrosa utopía habitable. Casa Son Vida es el primero de los seis proyectos progresivos planeados por Cosmopolitan Estates Ltd., con los que pretenden redefinir el estilo arquitectónico mediterráneo y situar Mallorca a la vanguardia del diseño internacional.

The bathrooms were decorated with Bisazza mosaics in a riot of colors, while geometric lines, open spaces, and wall structures create a futuristic pop-art landscape. Like all the hardware in the house, the fittings are state-of-the-art, some of them made to order.

Die Badezimmer wurden in einem Farbenrausch aus Bisazza-Mosaiken gestaltet. Grafische Linien, aufgebrochene Raumaufteilungen und Wandgestaltungen kreieren eine futuristische Popart-Landschaft. Die Armaturen sind wie die gesamte Ausstattung im Haus State-of-the-Art und wurden teilweise extra angefertigt.

En los baños se ha optado por una auténtica explosión de colores con mosaicos de Bisazza, que unidos a los grafismos lineales, la distribución de las habitaciones y los adornos murales componen un futurista paisaje pop-art. La grifería, al igual que el resto de instalaciones en la casa, es de excelente calidad, y algunas de las piezas han sido incluso creadas a medida.

Palacio Feliu

Palma de Mallorca

The Scandinavian owners of this 16th-century townhouse in Palma's historic center completely gutted the building and rebuilt it from the ground up over a period of many years. They turned the many small rooms of the original layout into spacious salons filled with light, integrated old structural elements such as archways and natural stone into the interior and rebuilt parts of the massive wooden ceilings using antique wood. The result exudes fresh elegance with a Mediterranean flair that flows through the entire building. The first floor is divided into a living room, kitchen, dining room and library, with bedrooms and ensuite bathrooms upstairs. The crowning glory is a rooftop terrace that puts a modern spin on a Bedouin tent, bringing the outdoors into the home.

Der Stadtpalast aus dem 16. Jahrhundert inmitten von Palmas Altstadt wurde von seinen skandinavischen Besitzern über mehrere Jahre völlig entkernt und von Grund auf neu gestaltet. Aus den vielen kleinen Zimmern der ursprünglichen Raumaufteilung sind großzügige lichtdurchflutete Säle entstanden. Alte Bauelemente wie Torbögen und Natursteine wurden in die Interieurs integriert und die massiven Holzdecken teilweise mit antikem Holz rekonstruiert. Das Ergebnis ist eine erfrischende Eleganz mit mediterranem Flair, die sich durch das gesamte Gebäude zieht. Die erste Etage teilt sich auf in Salon, Küche, Esszimmer und Bibliothek, darüber befinden sich die Schlafzimmer mit Badezimmern en suite. Den Abschluss bildet die Dachterrasse, die mit einer modernen Interpretation eines Beduinenzelts den Außenraum zum Innenraum macht.

El palacete del siglo XVI, situado en pleno centro del casco antiguo de Palma, tuvo que ser eviscerado por completo por sus propietarios escandinavos antes de ser remodelado por completo a lo largo de varios años. La multitud de habitacioncitas originales ha dado paso a una distribución mucho más amplia y luminosa. En el diseño de los interiores se han integrado los elementos arquitectónicos antiguos (umbrales, piedra vista...) y se ha procurado restaurar los macizos techos de madera con materiales antiguos. El resultado irradia frescor, elegancia y sabor mediterráneo. La primera planta acoge un salón, la cocina, el comedor y la biblioteca; más arriba se encuentran los dormitorios, todos dotados de baño propio. Corona el edificio la azotea, en la que una interpretación moderna de las jaimas beduinas convierte el exterior en un nuevo espacio interior.

The underlying color of the furnishings, which were designed by Rialto Living, is accented by different shades: red/pink in the living room, black in the library, and blue in the dining room. Antiques blend with modern elements, lending the house a timeless elegance.

Der helle Grundton der Einrichtung, die von Rialto Living gestaltet wurde, wird in den verschiedenen Bereichen durch unterschiedliche Farben akzentuiert: Rot/Pink im Salon, Schwarz in der Bibliothek und Blau im Esszimmer. Das Zusammenspiel von Antiquitäten und modernen Elementen verleiht dem Haus eine zeitlose Eleganz.

La luminosa paleta cromática de las instalaciones, concebida por Rialto Living, se acentúa en las distintas zonas con el recurso a colores diferentes: rojo/rosa en el salón, negro en la biblioteca y azul en el comedor. La combinación de antigüedades y piezas modernas confiere al conjunto un estilo elegante e intemporal.

SPENDING A LOT OF TIME

Ca'n Montesión

Palma de Mallorca

Built in 1753, this mansion stands in Palma's historic center. It was meticulously restored with a keen eye for the underlying historic features and equipped with cutting-edge technology. The spacious rooms were renovated to suit the owner's personal lifestyle and cover three floors, joined by several flights of stairs. The various areas offer space for an extensive collection of modern art. At the heart of the mansion lies the planta noble (the first floor), which contains a custom-made kitchen and adjacent dining room, a sitting room with a fireplace, and a home office/lounge. The golden antelopes—sculptures by Marios Elefteriades—add a surreal note to the regal yet modern ambiance. Large pictures and other objects hang from the ceiling, which rises nearly 23 feet overhead.

Mitten in Palmas Altstadt liegt dieser Stadtpalast von 1753, der mit viel Respekt vor der historischen Grundsubstanz aufwendig restauriert und mit modernster Technik ausgestattet wurde. Die großzügigen Räume, individuell auf den Lebensstil des Besitzers zugeschnitten und umgestaltet, verteilen sich auf drei Etagen, die durch mehrere Treppenaufgänge verbunden sind. In den einzelnen Bereichen findet sich Raum für die umfangreiche moderne Kunstsammlung. Die planta noble, die erste Etage, ist das Herzstück des Palastes. Hier befindet sich die maßgefertigte Küche mit anschließendem Esszimmer, Kaminsaal und Arbeits-Lounge-Salon. Die goldenen Antilopen, Skulpturen von Marios Elefteriades, geben dem modern-herrschaftlichen Ambiente etwas Surreales. Großformatige Bilder und andere Objekte hängen an den Wänden, die eine Höhe von fast sieben Metern haben.

En pleno casco antiguo de Palma se alza un palacete de 1753, restaurado con el más escrupuloso respeto por la estructura original y dotado con tecnología de vanguardia. Las espaciosas salas interiores, convenientemente adaptadas al estilo vida del propietario, se distribuyen sobre la superficie de tres plantas conectadas entre sí por varias escaleras. Las distintas zonas de la casa albergan una extensa colección de arte. El corazón del palacete, con todo, late en su planta noble: allí se encuentra una cocina diseñada a medida, así como el comedor, el hogar y un salón/*lounge*/cuarto de trabajo. Las esculturas de antílopes dorados, obra de Marios Elefteriades, aportan una nota de irrealidad al ambiente, moderno y señorial. Los casi siete metros de altura de los techos se han aprovechado para exponer cuadros de gran formato y otras piezas artísticas.

Oratorio de Sant Feliu

Palma de Mallorca

The gallery and private residence of Jule Kewenig is situated close to Paseo del Borne in Palma's historic center. The spacious apartment covers an entire floor. The reception area is filled with a harmonious blend of classic antique furniture from different historic periods, its quiet elegance dominated by an enormous upside down oil painting of the gallery owner by Georg Baselitz, who is also a personal friend. Additional works by Marcelo Viquez Bianqui and other artists as well as installations by Christian Boltanski lend a unique atmosphere to the interior with its tasteful wood paneling. The other rooms, located on a mezzanine, range from dining room to workroom to bedrooms. Once again, selected and highly distinctive decorative elements combine with Art Deco, Regency and Biedermeier furniture to create a harmonious backdrop.

Die Galerie und Privatwohnung der Galeristin Jule Kewenig liegt unweit des Paseo del Borne in Palmas Altstadt. Die weitläufige Wohnung erstreckt sich über eine gesamte Etage. Die ruhige Eleganz der Empfangsräume mit ihrer harmonischen Mischung aus klassischen antiken Möbeln verschiedener Zeitepochen wird von einem großformatigen Ölbild des befreundeten Künstlers Georg Baselitz dominiert, das die Hausherrin „über Kopf" zeigt. Weitere Werke, u. a. von Marcelo Viquez Bianqui, und Installationen von Christian Boltanski geben dem Interieur zusammen mit der gediegenen Holzvertäfelung eine einzigartige Atmosphäre. In einem Mezzanin befinden sich Esszimmer, Arbeitszimmer und Schlafzimmer. Auch hier verbinden sich die sehr akzentuiert ausgewählten Dekorationselemente mit dem Art-déco-, Regency- und Biedermeier-Mobiliar zu einer stimmigen Wohnkulisse.

La galería y residencia privada de la galerista Jule Kewenig se encuentra a poca distancia del Paseo del Borne, en el casco antiguo de Palma. La espaciosa vivienda ocupa una planta entera del edificio. Un cuadro de gran tamaño de su amigo y artista Georg Baselitz (en el que la dueña de la casa aparece cabeza abajo) domina el vestíbulo, de una serena elegancia nacida de la armoniosa combinación de muebles clásicos y antiguos de diversas épocas. El conjunto de piezas artísticas e instalaciones (de Marcelo Viquez Bianqui y Christian Boltanski, entre otros), enmarcado en los elegantes enmaderamientos de las paredes, crea un ambiente interior único. Las restantes salas se extienden a lo largo de una entreplanta: comedor, sala de trabajo y dormitorios. En todas ellas, una vez más , los selectos elementos decorativos se combinan con el mobiliario de estilo Art Déco, Regency y Biedermeier para componer un armónico espacio residencial.

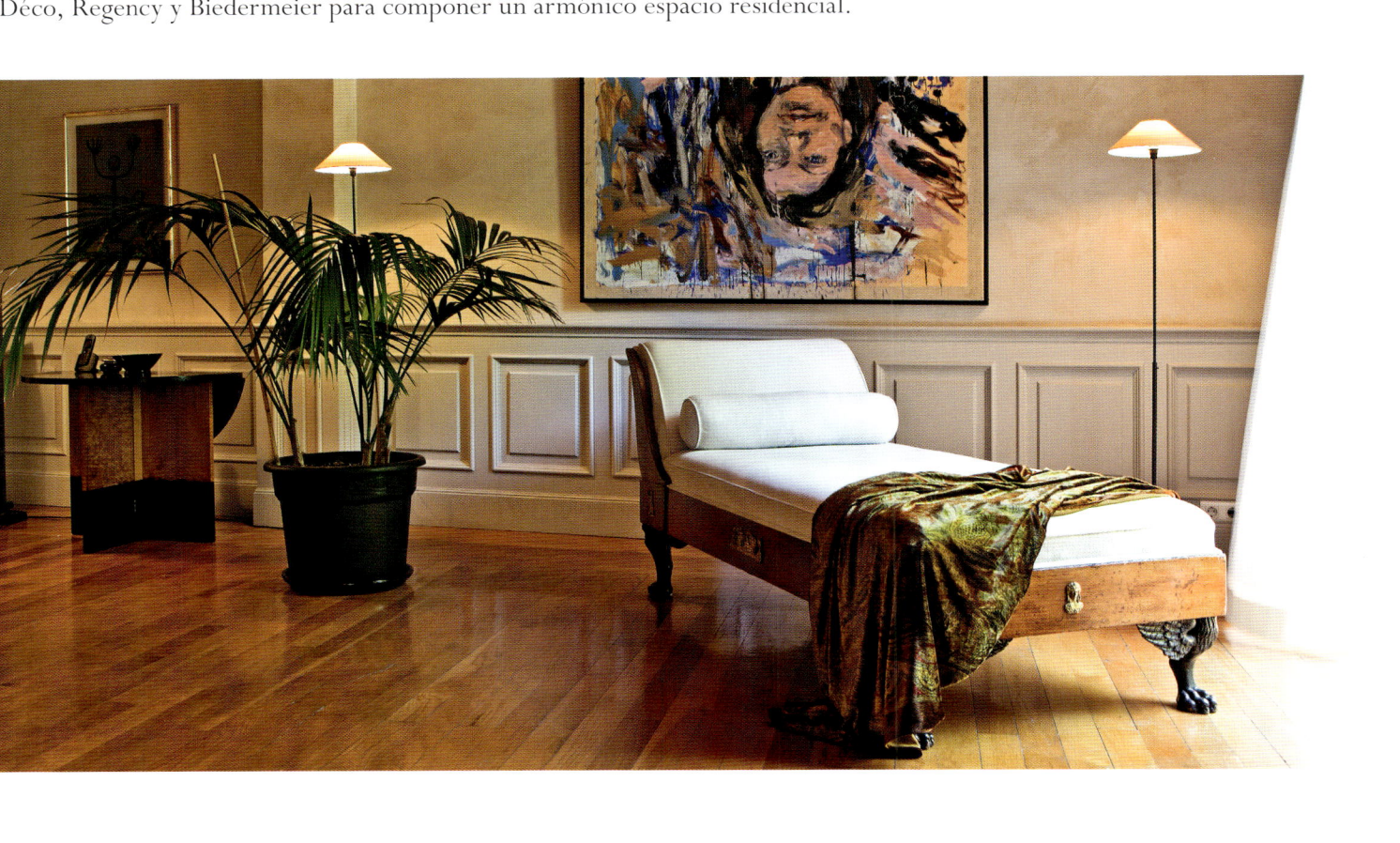

Lime-green fabrics, brilliantly-colored pictures and exquisite Fortuny lamps from Venice lend the master bedroom a Bohemian charm that harks back to an earlier century.

Dem Hauptschlafzimmer verleihen die lindgrünen Stoffe, farbexplosiven Bilder und erlesenen Fortuny-Lampen aus Venedig einen Bohemien-Charme aus einem anderen Jahrhundert.

El verde suave de las telas, unido a la estridencia cromática de los cuadros y las exquisitas lámparas venecianas Fortuny confieren al dormitorio principal el encanto bohemio de siglos pasados.

76   Oratorio de Sant Feliu

80   Oratorio de Sant Feliu

The former 13th-century chapel, with its original altar, is now a spectacular show room, where prominent artists exhibit their work.

Das Oratorio de Sant Feliu ist eine Kapelle aus dem 13. Jahrhundert, die mit ihrem Originalaltar ein eindrucksvoller Ausstellungsraum für renommierte Künstler ist.

En la antigua capilla del siglo XIII se conserva todavía el altar original; la sala es hoy un impresionante espacio de exposición en el que artistas de renombre presentan sus obras.

Palacio blanco-negro
Palma de Mallorca

This 19th-century palace is situated in the classiest part of Palma's historic center. A luxuriously elegant atmosphere fills 9,700 square feet of living space on four floors as well as a rooftop terrace. The house was completely renovated and redecorated by dai[10] arquitectura+interiorismo. Equipped with cutting-edge technology, the palacio nevertheless has preserved the elegance of an earlier age. The architects reinterpreted the house's history, using premium materials. The black-and-white color scheme sets the tone for the rooms with their 13-foot ceilings. Classic 20th- and 21st-century designs blend harmoniously with Louis XV decor and form the perfect backdrop for the owner's notable collection of contemporary art.

Der Palast aus dem 19. Jahrhundert liegt im nobelsten Teil von Palmas Altstadt. Über vier Stockwerke und eine Dachterrasse verteilen sich 900 Quadratmeter luxuriös-elegante Wohnatmosphäre. Das Haus wurde von dai[10] arquitectura + interiorismo vollständig saniert und neu dekoriert. Ausgestattet mit modernster Technik, hat es dennoch den herrschaftlichen Charakter alter Zeiten bewahrt. Mit den edlen Materialien wurde die Geschichte des Hauses neu interpretiert. Das schwarz-weiße Farbkonzept bestimmt den Grundcharakter der vier Meter hohen Räume. Designklassiker des 20. und 21. Jahrhunderts werden harmonisch mit Louis XV. gemischt und bieten den passenden Rahmen für die bedeutende Sammlung zeitgenössischer Kunst des Hausherrn.

El decimonónico palacio se ubica en la zona más noble del casco antiguo palmesano. A lo largo y ancho de sus 900 metros cuadrados, repartidos en cuatro plantas y una azotea, se extiende un ambiente a un tiempo lujoso y elegante. La casa fue completamente renovada y redecorada por dai[10] arquitectura+interiorismo. Dotada de la más moderna tecnología, ha conseguido sin embargo conservar el aire señorial de otras épocas. Los nobles materiales permiten una reinterpretación de la historia de la casa. El concepto en blanco y negro determina el carácter esencial de las distintas habitaciones, con techos de hasta cuatro metros de altura. Clásicos del diseño de los siglos XX y XXI conviven con muebles Luis XV y conforman el marco apropiado para la muy apreciable colección de arte contemporáneo del propietario.

The house centers around a patio and its vertical garden whose presence is felt throughout the building.

Den Mittelpunkt des Hauses bildet der Patio mit einem vertikalen Garten, der sich durch das gesamte Gebäude zieht.

El jardín vertical del patio es el eje en torno al cual se estructura todo el edificio.

Parliament Apartment

Palma de Mallorca

Situated in Palma's historic downtown, this late 18th-century building exudes French charm, which is why its new owners decided to lend a Parisian ambiance to the interior of their city home. They added four small balconies to the first floor of their stunning duplex, with its view of the Palma Cathedral, and stylishly combined antiques with classic furniture. Opulent crystal chandeliers, indigenous elements and modern art conspire to create a living space with a timeless international ambience. The upper floor contains a spacious lounge and the master bedroom. The entire front of this floor opens onto a large terrace that offers a spectacular panoramic view of the historic center, the harbor and the Mediterranean Sea.

Das inmitten der historischen Altstadt gelegene Gebäude aus dem späten 18. Jahrhundert hat französischen Charme, weshalb sich die neuen Eigentümer dafür entschieden, dem Interieur ihres Stadtdomizils eine Pariser Anmutung zu geben. Im unteren Geschoss des fantastischen Duplex' mit Blick auf Palmas Kathedrale befinden sich vier französische Balkone. Antiquitäten wurden stilvoll mit klassischen Möbeln kombiniert. Begleitet von opulenten Kristallleuchtern, ethnischen Elementen und moderner Kunst entstand so ein internationales, zeitloses Wohnambiente. Im oberen Bereich befinden sich ein weitläufiger Salon und das Hauptschlafzimmer. Die gesamte Vorderfront der Etage führt auf eine große Terrasse, die einen spektakulären Rundumblick auf die Altstadt, den Hafen und das Mittelmeer bietet.

El edificio, situado en el centro del casco histórico de la ciudad, fue construido en el siglo XVIII; de él emana un encanto afrancesado que animó a los propietarios a incorporar detalles parisinos a su residencia en la ciudad. En la planta baja de este fantástico dúplex con vistas a la catedral de Palma se abren cuatro balconcitos con amplias ventanas. Dentro, las antigüedades conviven con muebles clásicos en elegante armonía. El ambiente es internacional e intemporal, subrayado por opulentas arañas de cristal, detalles étnicos y piezas de arte moderno. En la planta superior se encuentran un espacioso salón y el dormitorio principal. Una terraza ocupa la parte frontal de la vivienda, desde la que es posible disfrutar espectaculares y amplísimas vistas sobre el casco antiguo, el mar y el puerto.

92   Parlament Apartment

Parlament Apartment 95

Ca'n Blau

Cala Llombards

Ca'n Blau puts a modern spin on the architectural style of Majorca's country homes, which are built in a horseshoe shape around an inner courtyard. Natural materials and sparse furnishings in natural colors with black accents lend the interior a meditative tranquility. Situated right on the coastal cliffs high above the Mediterranean Sea, the light-filled rooms with spectacular panoramic ocean views radiate pure elegance and transparency. With 3,000 square feet of living space, the house is surrounded by a Japanese Zen garden filled with art installations. A pool is harmoniously set into the patio and bordered by another decorative pool. The living/dining area and the kitchen are located in the center of the building. The four bedrooms with ensuite bathrooms are situated on each side of the house and provide direct access to the patio.

Ca'n Blau ist eine moderne Interpretation der Bauweise mallorquinischer Landsitze, bei denen die eingeschossigen Gebäude in Hufeisenform um einen Innenhof angelegt sind. Die Naturmaterialien und sparsam eingesetzten Einrichtungselemente in Naturfarben mit schwarzen Akzenten geben dem Interieur eine meditative Ruhe. Direkt an der Steilküste oberhalb des Mittelmeers gelegen, strahlen die lichtdurchfluteten Räume mit dem spektakulären Panoramablick auf das Meer eine schlichte Eleganz und Transparenz aus. Das Haus mit 290 Quadratmetern Wohnfläche ist von einem japanischen Zen-Garten mit Kunstinstallationen umgeben. Der harmonisch in die Terrasse eingelassene Pool wird von einem Zierpool begrenzt. Im Mittelteil des Baus befinden sich der Wohn- und Essbereich sowie die Küche. Die vier Schlafzimmer mit Badezimmern en suite verteilen sich auf die beiden Seitengebäude und haben direkten Zugang zum Patio.

Ca'n Blau es una reinterpretación moderna del estilo arquitectónico de las *possessions* mallorquinas, en las que los edificios de planta única se estructuran en forma de herradura en torno a un patio interior. Los materiales naturales y la moderación en el uso de elementos decorativos (de colores naturales, con apenas algunas pinceladas de negro) confieren al interior una serenidad que invita a la meditación. Situadas frente a los abruptos acantilados abiertos al Mediterráneo, cada una de las luminosas habitaciones goza de vistas espectaculares sobre las aguas e irradia elegancia y transparencia. Un jardín zen japonés rodea los 290 metros cuadrados de la casa; la piscina, que se adentra armoniosamente en la terraza, está limitada por un pequeño estanque ornamental. En la parte central del complejo se encuentran el salón y el comedor, así como la cocina. Los cuatro dormitorios, cada uno con baño propio, ocupan las dos naves laterales de la construcción y cuentan con acceso directo al patio.

Finca sa Pedra

Santanyí

The finca owned by the prominent Italian artist, Fabrizio Plessi, and his wife is an excellent example of the way historic structural elements can blend symbiotically with contemporary architecture. A modern structure was added to the original building, forming a harmonious whole. The old walls and rock fragments were integrated into the concrete floors and walls, and the furnishings were deliberately kept to a minimum. The resulting staged spaces show the artist's personal objects, sparse decor and monochrome furnishings to their full advantage. Light pours through large windows all over the house; after all, it was the special island light that motivated the owner to build his home here. At night, a specially-designed lighting system lends the spacious rooms a fairly hallowed atmosphere.

Die Finca des renommierten italienischen Künstlers Fabrizio Plessi und seiner Frau ist ein besonderes Beispiel für die Symbiose von historischen Bauelementen und moderner Architektur. An die vorhandene Bausubstanz wurde ein moderner Teil angefügt, der harmonisch mit dem Gebäude verschmilzt. Die alten Mauern und Felsfragmente wurden in die Betonböden und Wände integriert; die Einrichtung ist bewusst sparsam gehalten. In den so entstandenen und inszenierten Räumen kommen die Objekte des Künstlers, sowie die wenigen Dekorationen und monochromen Einrichtungsgegenstände, besonders gut zur Geltung. Überall durchflutet Licht die großen Fensterflächen und dieses besondere Licht der Insel war es auch, das den Hausherrn zum Bau bewegte. Nachts verleiht ein eigens angelegtes Lichtsystem den weitläufigen, klaren Räumen einen fast sakralen Charakter.

La finca del reputado artista italiano Fabrizio Plessi y su mujer es un magnífico ejemplo de simbiosis entre elementos arquitectónicos históricos y estética moderna. A la antigua estructura se le ha añadido un ala moderna que se funde armoniosamente en el edificio. Los muros y rocas antiguas se han integrado en los suelos de hormigón y en las paredes, y se ha optado por decorar el espacio de manera muy escueta. Los espacios resultantes permiten resaltar las líneas de las esculturas artísticas y las escasas piezas de mobiliario monocromo y de decoración. Los ventanales inundan de luz el interior; precisamente la luz tan especial de la isla fue la que inspiró la construcción de la finca. Por la noche, un sistema de iluminación muy especial confiere a las de por sí claras y espaciosas salas un carácter casi sacro.

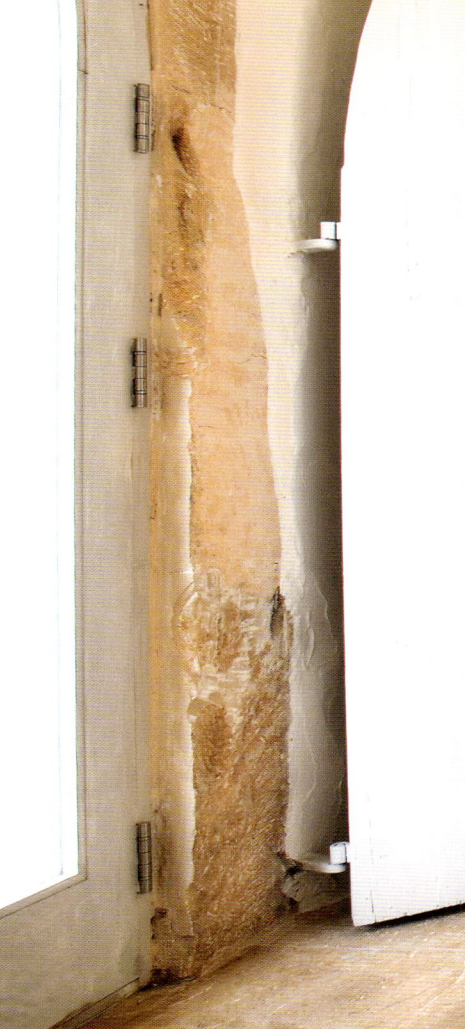

The homeowner describes his approach to interior design as a kind of "barbaric minimalism." The artist's intent is to offer a "profound homage to stone." The interior was designed to reflect the rocky and light-filled environment of this part of the island.

Als eine Art „barbarischen Minimalismus" beschreibt der Hausherr seinen Einrichtungsstil; der Künstler sieht hier eine „profunde Hommage an den Stein" umgesetzt. Das Interieur soll die steinige und lichtdurchflutete Umgebung dieses Teils der Insel widerspiegeln.

El propietario describe su estilo de interiorismo como una especie de «minimalismo bárbaro»: el artista ha llevado a la práctica un «profundo homenaje a la piedra». El interior de la casa pretende reflejar el entorno rocoso y bañado por la luz de esta parte de la isla.

In Fabrizio Plessi's mind, the genius loci, or spirit of the place, is what sets this house on Majorca apart from all his other homes around the world. And this spirit is found throughout the house's interior design.

Nach Fabrizio Plessi ist es vor allem der genius loci, der Geist des Ortes, der das Haus auf Mallorca von seinen anderen Domizilen auf der Welt unterscheidet. Und dieser Geist wird auch durch die Inszenierung des Interieurs wiedergegeben.

Si algo distingue su casa mallorquina de sus otras residencias, afirma Fabrizio Plessi, ese algo es el genius loci, el espíritu del lugar, un espíritu que se halla también muy presente en la configuración de los interiores.

Finca sa Pedra

Son Silvestre

Santanyí

The architecture of this country estate is a modern interpretation of a traditional Mediterranean manor. The heart of this home is the enormous central hall, which serves as both living and dining area. The imposing, 20-foot ceiling made of antique wood invokes the ceilings of Spanish palaces. The purist furnishings show the architecture to advantage; nothing distracts the eye from the clean lines. The fireplace in the main hall passes through the wall into the home office/lounge area and can be viewed from both rooms. With walls painted in a terra-cotta shade, this is the only part of the house that departs from the general color scheme. The extensive grounds, with their grid layout, consistently repeat the clear use of form and provide a heavenly ocean view.

In der Architektur dieses Landanwesens wurde das traditionelle mediterrane Herrenhaus modern umgesetzt. Kernstück ist die monumentale zentrale Halle, die als Salon und Esszimmer genutzt wird. Die imposante, sechs Meter hohe Deckenkonstruktion aus altem Holz zitiert die Decken spanischer Paläste. Die puristische Einrichtung lässt die Architektur voll zur Geltung kommen, nichts lenkt von der klaren Linienführung ab. Der Kamin in der Haupthalle geht durch die Wand in den Arbeits- und Loungebereich des Hauses über und ist so von beiden Räumen aus zu betrachten. Dies ist der einzige Bereich des Hauses, der mit seiner Terrakotta-Wandfarbe das helle Farbkonzept des Hauses bricht. Die grafisch angelegten großflächigen Außenanlagen führen die klare Formensprache konsequent fort und bieten einen traumhaften Weitblick bis aufs Meer.

Para la construcción de esta villa rural se optó por una reinterpretación moderna de la tradicional casa señorial mediterránea. El conjunto gira en torno a la gran sala central, que hace las veces de salón y comedor. Los imponentes techos, de seis metros de altura y construidos en madera, evocan los de otros palacios españoles. El purista interiorismo resalta particularmente la sencilla grandeza del diseño: nada distrae la mirada de la claridad de trazo. La chimenea de la sala principal comparte pared con la zona de reposo y trabajo de la casa, y resulta visible desde ambas habitaciones. Esta es la única zona de la casa en la que el color terracota de las paredes rompe el claro esquema cromático de la casa. Las gráficas instalaciones exteriores suponen la continuación de la claridad formal interior y ofrecen una panorámica de ensueño sobre las aguas del Mediterráneo.

Grimalt Charming
Santanyí

Built in the classic Majorcan finca style, this country home exudes an entirely unpretentious, close-to-nature charm. The English owner and his wife were enchanted by the peaceful atmosphere surrounding the once derelict building and embraced the idea of turning the place into an authentic, Mediterranean retreat. The simple, whitewashed interior radiates pure tranquility, while the traditional Majorcan rocking chairs and antique farm implements that decorate the entrance lend a hint of regional authenticity. With a keen eye for traditional elements, the owners created a contemporary atmosphere with an open kitchen and spacious, light-filled areas that reflect the owner's credo: "room, light and tranquility are real luxuries."

Dieses Landhaus im klassisch-mallorquinischen Fincastil hat einen besonders unprätentiösen und naturverbundenen Charme. Der englische Eigentümer und seine Frau waren bezaubert von der friedvollen Atmosphäre, die das ehemals verfallene Gebäude umgab, und begeistert von der Idee, hier einen authentischen mediterranen Rückzugsort zu schaffen. Das schlichte, weiß gekalkte Interieur strahlt eine wohltuende Ruhe aus, und die inseltypischen Schaukelstühle und antiken landwirtschaftlichen Geräte, die den Eingangsbereich dekorieren, schaffen regionale Bezüge. Mit viel Feingefühl für traditionelle Elemente wurde eine zeitgemäße Wohnatmosphäre geschaffen, die mit der offenen Küche und der großzügigen, lichtdurchfluteten Raumaufteilung dem Credo des Hausherrn folgt: „Raum, Licht und Stille sind der wahre Luxus".

Esta clásica finca mallorquina derrocha un encanto natural, carente por completo de pretensiones. La serena atmósfera que rodea al otrora ruinoso edificio cautivó a su actual propietario británico y a su esposa, esto les animó a crear un auténtico refugio mediterráneo a partir de aquellos mimbres. El sencillo y enjalbegado interior irradia serenidad, y las mecedoras típicas de la isla y los aperos de labranza que decoran la entrada acentúan el arraigo en la región. Se ha sabido crear un entorno residencial contemporáneo prestando especial atención a los elementos tradicionales, como la cocina abierta y la espaciosa y luminosísima distribución de los espacios, fiel al credo del propietario: «El espacio, la luz y el silencio son el verdadero lujo».

Natural Conclusion
Santanyí

Sculptor Dörte Wehmeyer selected the barren, rocky landscape of southeastern Majorca as the site for her island hideaway. The house fits in harmoniously with the surrounding landscape, and a building made of natural stone, glass and steel was added to the existing structure. Using environmentally-friendly technologies, the builder created an oasis that blends in with its natural surroundings. Except for a vintage deck lounge from England, all the furnishings were made on the island. The owner chose to do without color throughout the building, and only understated natural shades and natural materials were used for the minimalist interior decor, creating an inviting and relaxed atmosphere. The bathrooms and kitchen use the natural stone found in the surrounding nature, which makes for clean, esthetic lines.

Die karge, steinige Landschaft im Südosten Mallorcas hat die Bildhauerin Dörte Wehmeyer bewusst als Standort für ihr Refugium auf der Insel ausgewählt. Das Haus ist harmonisch in die umliegende Landschaft eingebettet, an einen bereits bestehenden Teil wurde eine Konstruktion aus Naturstein, Glas und Stahl angefügt. Unter besonderer Berücksichtigung ökologischer Technologien ist so eine Oase entstanden. Außer einem Vintage-Liegestuhl aus England stammt die gesamte Einrichtung von der Insel. Im ganzen Gebäude wurde auf Farben verzichtet, die sparsam dekorierten Interieurs sind in zurückhaltenden Naturtönen und -materialien gehalten, wodurch ein freundliches und entspanntes Ambiente entsteht. Der Naturstein aus der Umgebung findet sich im Haus auch in den Bädern und der Küche wieder und sorgt für eine klare gestalterische Linie.

La escultora Dörte Wehmeyer se decantó conscientemente por el paisaje desabrido y pedregoso del sudeste mallorquín para construir su refugio en la isla. La casa se integra a la perfección en su entorno: a la estructura ya existente se le ha añadido otra construida en piedra, vidrio y acero. Ateniéndose estrictamente al uso de tecnologías ecológicas ha surgido así un oasis en completa armonía con la naturaleza que lo rodea. Excepción hecha de una tumbona *vintage* inglesa, todos los interiores son de origen mallorquín. Se ha renunciado al uso del color en el edificio, y los espacios interiores, escasamente decorados, se han mantenido en tonos y materiales naturales, lo que engendra un ambiente acogedor y relajado. La piedra natural del entorno está presente en los baños y la cocina, y contribuye en buena medida a la claridad estética que domina el conjunto.

126　Natural Conclusion

Natural Conclusion 129

Casa Neuendorf

Santanyí

Resembling a minimalistic medieval castle, the home of art dealer Hans Neuendorf is surrounded by the characteristic red, rocky soil of southern Majorca. With its geometric, purist architecture, the house was one of the first buildings on the island to be built in such a rectilinear style. This masterpiece of Mediterranean minimalism was built in 1991 by the John Pawson & Claudio Silvestrin architecture firm. The austere, plain facade made of natural stone blends harmoniously with its surroundings, whose colors are repeated in the building's exterior. The 6,500 square feet of living space open onto a patio with a pool surrounded by typical Mediterranean vegetation. Visitors enter the property along a perfectly straight, 361-foot stone walkway.

Einer minimalistischen mittelalterlichen Burg gleich steht das Haus des Kunsthändlers Hans Neuendorf inmitten der charakteristischen roten, felsigen Erde im südlichen Teil Mallorcas. Mit seiner geometrisch-puristischen Architektur war es einer der ersten Bauten der Insel, der sich einer derart geradlinigen Ästhetik bediente. Dieses Meisterwerk des mediterranen Minimalismus wurde 1991 errichtet und stammt aus dem Hause des Architektenduos John Pawson & Claudio Silvestrin. Das Landanwesen fügt sich mit seiner strengen, klaren Fassade aus Naturstein harmonisch in die Umgebung ein. Die 600 Quadratmeter Wohnfläche führen auf einen Patio und den von typischer Mittelmeervegetation umgebenen Pool. Zum Eingang wird der Besucher auf einem 110 Meter langen, schnurgeraden Steinweg geführt.

Cual minimalista castillo medieval, la casa del marchante de arte Hans Neuendorf se alza sobre el característico terreno rojizo y pedregoso del sur mallorquín. El purismo geométrico de sus formas hace del edificio uno de los primeros en valerse de tan rectilínea estética en la isla. Esta obra maestra del minimalismo mediterráneo fue construida en 1991 y es obra del dúo de arquitectos John Pawson & Claudio Silvestrin. Las líneas estrictas y claras de la fachada la integran armoniosamente en su entorno, al que también se adaptan sus colores. Los 600 metros cuadrados de superficie habitable conducen a un patio y a la piscina, rodeada de vegetación típicamente mediterránea. Un sendero de 110 metros en línea recta conduce al visitante hasta la entrada.

The strictly minimalistic furnishings create a cool and soberly restful atmosphere with carefully selected and placed examples of classic modern design.

Konsequent sparsam ist die Einrichtung, die mit der gezielten Auswahl und Platzierung von modernen Designklassikern eine kühle und sachlich-ruhige Stimmung schafft.

En el interior se ha optado por un estilo sobrio que, unido a la excelente selección y distribución de clásicos del diseño moderno, acaba por crear un ambiente sereno y objetivo.

136   Casa Neuendorf

You look out through a small number of narrow, low-lying window openings that frame the view.

Der Blick nach draußen wird durch wenige schmale und tiefliegende Fensteröffnungen freigegeben, welche die Aussicht wie gerahmt erscheinen lassen.

Unas pocas ventanas estrechas y profundas abren el edificio al exterior y enmarcan las vistas.

Casa Neuendorf

Son Almendros

Cas Concos

This modern country home, with its double staircase, resembles a Mayan pyramid and was built in a joint effort between the Hamburg-based owner, Thomas Wegner, and Spanish architects, who worked from his designs. The building's rustic minimalism and an unusual waterfall, with water flowing from the second floor to an integrated pool, give the estate its unique atmosphere. Here and there, serendipitous discoveries and deliberately placed objects complement the Spartan interior design. The tranquility and almost formal simplicity of the interior provide an ideal space for the numerous contemporary paintings and objects from the owner's notable art collection. The two outdoor staircases lead to a rooftop terrace which has an 360-degree panoramic view of the mountains and the sea.

Das moderne Landhaus, das mit seiner dualen Treppenkonstruktion an eine Maya-Pyramide erinnert, ist das Ergebnis der Zusammenarbeit des Hamburger Hausherrn Thomas Wegner mit spanischen Architekten, die seine Entwürfe umsetzten. Der rustikale Minimalismus und die ungewöhnliche Wasserfallkonstruktion, die das Wasser aus dem ersten Stock in den integrierten Pool fließen lässt, geben dem Anwesen seinen einzigartigen Charakter. Vereinzelt ergänzen unerwartete Trouvaillen und gezielt platzierte Objekte die spartanische Inneneinrichtung. Die Ruhe und fast feierliche Klarheit der Innenräume bietet eine optimale Fläche für die zahlreichen zeitgenössischen Gemälde und Objekte aus der bedeutenden Kunstsammlung des Besitzers. Zwei Außentreppen führen auf eine Dachterrasse mit 360-Grad-Panorama-Blick auf die Berge und das Meer.

Esta moderna construcción, cuya doble escalera exterior recuerda en parte las pirámides mayas, es el resultado de la colaboración entre el constructor Thomas Wegner, de Hamburgo, y los arquitectos españoles que llevaron a la práctica sus diseños. El minimalismo rural del edificio, así como la llamativa cascada que se precipita desde el primer piso en la piscina integrada del recinto, confieren a la propiedad un carácter inconfundible. La austeridad del diseño interior se ve interrumpida solo por inesperados hallazgos y objetos decorativos estratégicamente dispuestos. La serenidad y la claridad casi alegre de los espacios interiores ofrecen el entorno ideal para la destacada colección de pintura y escultura moderna del propietario. Las dos escaleras exteriores conducen a una azotea con vistas panorámicas a la montaña y el mar.

The in-floor heaters installed throughout the house and the outer walls, which are twice as thick as usual, create a perfect year-round climate in the home. No matter what season it is, the temperatures are always ideal even without air-conditioning.

Die im ganzen Haus verlegte Fußbodenheizung und die Mauerkonstruktionen, die doppelt so dick sind wie sonst üblich, erzeugen im Haus das perfekte Ganzjahresklima. Auch ohne Klimaanlage sind die Temperaturen das ganze Jahr über immer optimal.

El suelo radiante instalado en toda la casa y el doble grosor de los muros permiten mantener un clima perfecto durante todo el año en el interior de la casa. Pero la temperatura es ideal todo el año, incluso sin aire acondicionado ni calefacción.

Son Almendros

Son Almendros 147

La Ruina
S'Horta

The ruins, which are between 250 and 450 years old, were meticulously restored by the owner, Thomas Wegner, over a period of three years. He took special care to preserve the original building sections and integrate them into the overall home. The exposed, crumbling wall structures that peak out from between the plasterwork and purist decor, give one the sense of having caught a glimpse of the house's soul. The entrance hall is between 13 and 26 feet high—and right in keeping with this ambiance, the atmospheric dedication ceremony featured an opera singer. Gravel from a nearby riverbed was used for the traditional floors in the downstairs areas, and a pool, integrated harmoniously into the garden landscape, is lined with black tiles to simulate water on the open ocean.

Die zwischen 250 und 450 Jahre alte Ruine wurde vom Eigentümer Thomas Wegner drei Jahre lang aufwendig restauriert. Dabei legte er besondere Sorgfalt auf den Erhalt der alten Gebäudeteile, die überall in das Haus integriert wurden. Durch die offenliegenden, zerfallenen Mauerkonstruktionen, die zwischen Putz und puristischen Einrichtungselementen hervorschauen, hat man das Gefühl, die Seele des Hauses zu sehen. Die Eingangshalle ist zwischen vier und acht Meter hoch – zu ihrer stimmungsvollen Einweihung wurde eine Opernsängerin engagiert. Für den traditionellen Boden der unteren Bereiche verwendete man Kieselsteine aus dem nahe gelegenen Flussbett, und der harmonisch in die Gartenlandschaft eingelassene Pool ist schwarz gekachelt, um das Wasser auf offener See nachzuempfinden.

Thomas Wegner, el actual propietario, dedicó tres laboriosos años a la restauración de esta ruina, de entre 250 y 450 años de antigüedad. En el proceso prestó especial atención a la conservación de los restos del antiguo edificio, integrados ahora en el conjunto de la casa. Los muros abiertos y semiderruidos que se entrevén bajo el enlucido y los puristas elementos de interiorismo crean la impresión de que se asoma uno al alma misma del edificio. El recibidor tiene techos de entre cuatro y ocho metros de altura: para la inauguración del edificio se contrataron muy atinadamente los servicios de una cantante de ópera. Para los tradicionales suelos de la planta inferior se han utilizado guijarros del torrente cercano, y la piscina, armónicamente insertada en la zona ajardinada, ha sido alicatada con baldosas negras para reproducir los colores del agua en mar abierto.

La Ruina 151

The harmonious blend of natural materials and high-quality engineering, and the interplay between white and natural hues, interrupted only by black accents, lend the rooms their tranquility and timeless appearance. Gilded mirrors add an unwavering opulence to the modern bathrooms, decorated in natural black stone.

Die harmonische Mischung aus Naturmaterialien und hochwertiger Technik und das Zusammenspiel von Weiß mit Naturtönen, das nur von schwarzen Details unterbrochen wird, verleiht den Räumen ihre Ruhe und zeitlose Ästhetik. Die modernen Bäder in schwarzem Naturstein bekommen durch die vergoldeten Spiegel eine strenge und klare Opulenz.

La armoniosa combinación de materiales naturales y la mejor tecnología, unida a un sabio contraste de blancos y tonos naturales, complementado con algunas pinceladas de negro, determina la estética atemporal y la serenidad de las distintas habitaciones. El dorado de los espejos confiere a los modernos baños de piedra natural negra una estricta y luminosa opulencia.

La Ruina 155

Son Llodra

Porto Christo

Dating back to the 17th century, this country home is embedded in the picturesque mountain landscape between Porto Cristo and Porto Colom. A blend of exquisite building materials, rural elements and whitewashed walls combines with casual elegance to form a timeless interior that reflects both international style and familial distinction. The finca is the private residence of the architect, Wolf Siegfried Wagner, and his wife, the interior designer, Eleonore von Haeften. Working with Wagner's W.S.W Arquitectura firm, the couple restored the property over twenty years ago. With typical hand-laid pebbles in the entrance, hand-crafted azulejos—antique tiles typical of the region—in the spacious open kitchen and old ceiling beams, Son Llodra is a hideaway that combines Mediterranean charm with international grandeur.

Das Landhaus mit Ursprung im 17. Jahrhundert liegt malerisch in den Bergen eingebettet zwischen Porto Cristo und Porto Colom. Die Mischung aus exquisiten Baustoffen, ländlichen Elementen und den geweißten Wänden verbindet sich mit der lässig-eleganten Einrichtung zu einem zeitlosen Interieur mit internationalem Stil und familiär-repräsentativem Charakter. Die Finca ist das Privathaus und Gemeinschaftsprojekt des Architekten Wolf Siegfried Wagner und seiner Frau, der Inneneinrichterin Eleonore von Haeften. Zusammen mit Wagners Firma W.S.W Arquitectura haben die beiden das Anwesen vor über 20 Jahren restauriert. Mit den typischen handverlegten Kieselsteinen im Eingangsbereich, den handgearbeiteten azulejos – den antiken Kacheln der Region – in der großzügigen Wohnküche und den alten Deckenbalken ist Son Llodra ein Refugium mit mediterranem Charme und internationaler Grandezza.

La finca tiene sus orígenes en el siglo XVII y se encuentra en un espacio privilegiado de las montañas entre Porto Cristo y Porto Colom. La combinación de exquisitos materiales, elementos rurales y encaladas paredes traza una línea que enlaza con la atemporalidad del interior, de estilo internacional y marcado carácter, a un tiempo familiar e imponente. La finca es la residencia privada del arquitecto Wolf Siegfried Wagner y su esposa, la interiorista Eleonore von Haeften. En cooperación con el despacho W.S.W Arquitectura del propio Wagner, ambos han dedicado 20 años a la restauración de la propiedad. El típico suelo de guijarros de la zona de acceso, los azulejos artesanales de la espaciosa cocina y las antiquísimas vigas del techo hacen de Son Llodra un refugio con encanto mediterráneo y *grandezza* internacional.

The large building complex is surrounded by magnificent, lush landscaping with an ocean view, park-like grounds, and an elegant pool area. The old-growth trees provide shade and give the residents a sense of seclusion.

Die weitläufige Gebäudeanlage ist umgeben von einer prachtvollen üppigen Gartenlandschaft mit Meeresblick, parkähnlichen Außenanlagen und einem eleganten Poolbereich. Der alte Baumbestand spendet Schatten und gibt den Bewohnern ein Gefühl der Abgeschiedenheit.

Los extensos edificios están rodeados por excepcionales zonas ajardinadas con vistas al mar, terrenos que en muchos casos recuerdan un parque y una elegante piscina. Los árboles de la propiedad ofrecen sombra y cobijo y aportan la sensación de vivir apartados del mundo.

Son Moix

Manacor

Dennis Wunderlich, owner of this recently built finca, designed the home together with his Spanish architects. The architecture has a streamlined, modern appearance whose linearity is as eye-catching as the strictly geometric layout of the landscaping. The house was designed with sustainability in mind. The angled flat roof has integrated solar panels that are hidden from view, and rain water is collected to irrigate the on-site vineyard, olive trees, and vegetable garden. The horseshoe-shaped house has a main hall, designed as a loft, with an imposing fenestrated facade, stretching 39 feet high, and two cube-shaped wings. The latter contain the two bedroom suites, one decorated in black and coal-gray for the master of the house and the other in cream and ivory for his lady. The masculine undertone is softened by Asian accents, with space organized according to Feng Shui criteria.

Die neu erbaute Finca wurde vom Eigentümer Dennis Wunderlich zusammen mit seinen spanischen Architekten gestaltet. Die klare, moderne Ästhetik der Architektur ist dabei in ihrer Geradlinigkeit genauso beeindruckend wie die ebenfalls streng grafisch angelegte mediterrane Gartenlandschaft. Das Haus wurde mit Hinblick auf Nachhaltigkeit konzipiert: Auf dem schrägen Flachdach sind unsichtbar Solarzellen integriert und das aufgefangene Regenwasser wird zur Bewässerung des hauseigenen Weines, der Oliven und des Gemüsegartens verwendet. Das u-förmige Gebäude teilt sich auf in die loftartige Haupthalle mit einer imposanten Fensterfront von zwölf Metern und zwei flankierende Kuben. Hier befinden sich die beiden Schlafsuiten – in Schwarz-Anthrazit gehalten für den Herrn, in Creme-Elfenbein für die Dame des Hauses. Die maskuline Grundstimmung wurde mit asiatischen Elementen akzentuiert, der Raum nach Feng-Shui-Kriterien aufgeteilt.

La finca, de reciente construcción, ha sido un proyecto conjunto del propietario Dennis Wunderlich y sus arquitectos españoles. La claridad de trazo de su modernísima estética resulta tan impresionante como los terrenos ajardinados circundantes, inconfundiblemente mediterráneos pero también sometidos a estrictas líneas. La residencia fue concebida prestando especial atención a la sostenibilidad: sobre la azotea se han instalado paneles solares ocultos a la vista, y el agua de lluvia se recoge y aprovecha para el riego de las viñas, los olivos y el huerto de la casa. El edificio, en forma de U, consta de una nave principal/loft con unos ventanales de 12 metros de ancho, flanqueada por dos cubos. En ellos se encuentran los dos dormitorios: negro antracita para él, color marfil/crema para ella. La masculinidad del ambiente se ve acentuada por los elementos de decoración asiáticos: el *feng shui* determina la distribución de espacios.

The floor is made of coal-gray microcement that visually links the different areas of the home. The dominant natural shades and materials used for the interior design are accented in black, which lends a Zen-like ambience.

Der Boden besteht aus anthrazitfarbenem Mikrozement und verbindet die einzelnen Bereiche des Hauses optisch miteinander. Die dominierenden Naturtöne und -materialien der Einrichtung werden durch Schwarz ergänzt und verleihen ein Zen-Ambiente.

El suelo, construido con microcemento de color antracita, sirve de ligazón óptica entre las distintas dependencias de la casa. En la decoración predominan las tonalidades y los materiales naturales, complementados aquí y allá por toques de negro: el conjunto crea una innegable atmósfera zen.

The large, airy living quarters, with their slightly sloping ceiling, accommodate the dining area, lounge, multimedia center and an open kitchen in 2,200 square feet of space. 92-feet long, with a window covering one entire wall, this room feels like you are sitting in a space that is open to the outdoors.

Die luftige Wohnhalle mit der leicht schrägen Deckenkonstruktion verbindet auf 200 Quadratmetern Essbereich, Salon, Multimedia-Bereich und eine offene Küche. Der Raum erstreckt sich über eine Länge von 28 Metern und gibt einem durch die vollflächige Fensterseite das Gefühl, in einem nach außen offenen Raum zu sitzen.

La espaciosísima sala, de techo ligeramente abuhardillado, acoge en sus 200 metros cuadrados de superficie comedor, salón, área multimedia y una cocina abierta. Se extiende a lo largo de 28 metros y gracias al ventanal que ocupa al completo uno de los laterales crea la impresión de estar completamente abierta al exterior.

Sa Canova
Artà

Restored by architect José Ferragut and featuring a 14th-century fortified tower, this country estate is owned by one of Majorca's oldest families. The interior design combines sandstone and natural stone from Binissalem with plasterwork, glass and steel. The gallery's steel and glass construction provides a stunning backdrop for antiques and original paintings from different historical periods. A large Italian designer table seats 20 people and has wooden chairs in gold and white that date back to the late 17th century. The golden Spanish columns from the 18th century frame a Spanish still life. Two cabinets displaying Chinese porcelain stand at one end of the great hall, beneath a painting by Paolo Anesi. The two portraits of the owner's ancestors in the foyer are some of the most valuable paintings in his large, unique collection.

Das Landanwesen mit einem Wehrturm aus dem 14. Jahrhundert ist im Besitz einer der ältesten Familien Mallorcas und wurde kürzlich vom Architekten José Ferragut restauriert. Beim Innenausbau wurden Sandstein, Naturstein aus Binissalem, Stucco, Glas und Stahl verwendet. Die Stahl- und Glaskonstruktion der Galerie bildet einen spannenden Kontrast zu den Kostbarkeiten des Interieurs, die aus wertvollen Antiquitäten und Originalgemälden verschiedener Epochen bestehen. Der große italienische Designertisch bietet Platz für 20 Personen, die gold-weißen Holzstühle stammen aus dem späten 17. Jahrhundert. Die goldenen spanischen Säulen aus dem 18. Jahrhundert rahmen ein spanisches Stillleben ein. Die Stirnseite des Saals wird unter einem Gemälde von Paolo Anesi von zwei Konsolen mit chinesischem Porzellan eingefasst. Unter den vielen einzigartigen Gemälden der Sammlung des Besitzers gehören die beiden Porträts seiner Vorfahren in der Eingangshalle zu den wertvollsten.

Inconfundible gracias a su torre de defensa del siglo XIV, la finca es propiedad de una de las familias con más abolengo de Mallorca y fue restaurada por el arquitecto José Ferragut, que recurrió a la arenisca, la piedra natural de Binissalem, el estuco, el vidrio y el acero para configurar los espacios interiores. La estructura de vidrio y acero de la galería ofrece un marcado contraste con las antigüedades y cuadros originales de distintas épocas. La enorme mesa italiana de diseño puede acoger hasta a 20 comensales, a los que esperan sillas de madera en blanco y oro de finales del siglo XVII. Dos columnas doradas del siglo XVIII flanquean un bodegón español. Un cuadro de Paolo Anesi y dos consolas con porcelana china enmarcan el frontal de la sala. De entre las muchas piezas que componen la colección del propietario, los retratos de sus antepasados que adornan el vestíbulo se cuentan entre las más preciadas.

Sa Canova 179

Es Puig

Artà

The interior of this recently built finca in the rugged northern part of the island is a particularly exciting mixture of African and Moorish style elements. The natural color scheme throughout the home continues in the vintage leather furniture and the warm-toned wood floor, interrupted only by Oriental-styled fabrics, carpets and antique decor. This classic country home of a Spanish architect and his family was designed and built by Bastidas Architects. The geometric layout of the grounds gives the house a modern appearance, despite its traditional floor plan. The library and mirrors were made to measure in Morocco, and the antique doors also come from this North African country. The black fireplace is rendered in tadelakt—a Moroccan form of Venetian plaster. African photographic images and masks emphasize the underlying ethnic ambience.

Eine Mischung aus afrikanischen und maurischen Stilelementen macht das Interieur dieser neu gebauten Finca im rauen Norden der Insel besonders spannend. Die durchgängigen Naturtöne werden von den Vintage-Ledermöbeln und dem warmen Holzboden aufgenommen und nur durchbrochen von den orientalisch anmutenden Stoffen, Teppichen und antiken Dekors. Das klassische Landhaus eines spanischen Architekten und seiner Familie wurde von Bastidas Architects entworfen und fertiggestellt. Die grafische Einteilung des Terrains gibt dem Haus trotz traditionellem Grundriss eine moderne Optik. Die Bibliothek und die Spiegel wurden in Marokko maßgefertigt, die antiken Türen stammen ebenfalls von dort. Der schwarze Kamin wurde mit Tadelakt – einer Art marokkanischem Stucco Veneziano – verputzt. Die afrikanischen Fotomotive und Masken unterstreichen die ethnische Grundnote.

La mezcla de elementos africanos y moriscos dota de un especial interés la zona interior de esta finca de reciente construcción, ubicada en el agreste norte de la isla. Las tonalidades naturales encuentran eco en los muebles *vintage* de cuero y los cálidos suelos de madera, y se ven interrumpidos solo por telas, alfombras y otros elementos decorativos de aire oriental. La clásica residencia rural de un arquitecto español y su familia fue diseñada y construida por Bastidas Architects. La distribución gráfica del terreno confiere una óptica moderna al conjunto, pese a lo tradicional de su plano. Las librerías y espejos fueron construidos a medida en Marruecos, y también las antiquísimas puertas son de origen marroquí. La negra chimenea está revocada con *tadelakt*, una especie de estuco marroquí. Las máscaras y fotografías con motivos africanos subrayan el ambiente étnico del conjunto.

Brightly-colored Berber carpets in the nursery emphasize the home's nomadic ambience. Moroccan accents and fabrics in the TV room, as well as the antique, hand-painted doors, create a cozy warmth, Maghreb-style. The large photo mounted on the wall depicts a North African colonnade and provides an attractive modern contrast.

Das Nomadenambiente des Hauses wird im Kinderzimmer durch die farbenfrohen Berberteppiche unterstrichen. Im Fernsehzimmer sorgen marokkanische Stilelemente und Stoffe sowie die antiken, handbemalten Türen für orientalische Behaglichkeit. Das groß aufgezogene Foto eines nordafrikanischen Wandelgangs bildet hierzu einen attraktiven modernen Kontrast.

El aire nómada de la casa tiene su reflejo en las coloristas alfombras bereberes del dormitorio de los niños. En el cuarto de la televisión, diversas telas y elementos decorativos marroquíes y unas antiguas puertas decoradas artesanalmente aportan la nota hogareña y oriental. Una fotografía de gran tamaño de una galería norteafricana ofrece en el contexto un atractivo y moderno contraste.

Ses Eres III
Artà

This recently built country estate in the northeastern part of the island recreates the contemporary style of a modern Mexican hacienda. A linear structural design and open architecture divide the outdoor areas into typical shady patios, terraces, dining and lounge areas—in keeping with the Mediterranean tradition. The surrounding terraces and a pergola provide a panoramic view of the landscape, all the way to the sea. Except for the facade's repeated terra-cotta color, the interior features only natural shades, and the ethnic decor elements form a stylish symbiosis with the unpretentiously classic, modern furniture. The restful color scheme is interrupted only by the confidently stylish black accents of the art objects, masks, and African wood.

Der neugebaute Landsitz im Nordosten der Insel ist dem zeitgenössischen Stil einer modernen mexikanischen Hazienda nachempfunden. Mit geradliniger Bauweise und offen gestalteter Architektur werden die Außenbereiche, der Mittelmeertradition folgend, in typische schattige Patios, Terrassenplätze, Ess- und Loungebereiche unterteilt. Von den umlaufenden Terrassenanlagen und der Pergola hat man einen Panoramablick auf die Landschaft bis hin zum Meer. Das Interieur ist bis auf die wiederkehrende Terrakottafarbe der Fassade in Naturtönen gehalten, und die ethnischen Dekorationselemente gehen mit den zurückgenommenen klassisch-modernen Möbeln eine stilvolle Symbiose ein. Unterbrochen wird die ruhige Farbstimmung nur durch die stilsicher eingesetzten schwarzen Farbakzente der Kunstgegenstände, Masken und afrikanischen Hölzer.

La propiedad, situada en el nordeste de la isla, ha sido edificada en el estilo contemporáneo de las modernas haciendas mexicanas. El trazo rectilíneo del diseño y los espacios abiertos propios de la tradición arquitectónica mediterránea estructura la zona exterior en típicos patios sombreados, terrazas, comedor y *lounge*. Desde la terraza que rodea el edificio y la pérgola pueden disfrutarse vistas panorámicas que se extienden hasta el mar. El interior mantiene una paleta de colores naturales (excepción hecha de los tonos terracota de la fachada) y los elementos étnicos de decoración combinan bien en elegante simbiosis con el clasicismo moderno y reservado de los muebles. La serenidad cromática del conjunto solo se ve interrumpida por las pinceladas de negro que aportan varias piezas artísticas, máscaras y maderas africanas.

Natural materials such as marès sandstone and exquisite home textiles complement each other harmoniously. Combined with the highest standards of comfort, they create a timeless, international ambience.

Naturmaterialien wie Marès und edle Wohntextilien ergänzen sich harmonisch. In Verbindung mit höchsten Komfortstandards ist hier ein zeitlos-internationales Wohnambiente entstanden.

Las materias primas como la piedra de marès y las nobles telas armonizan a la perfección, y unidas al extraordinario grado de confort alcanzado resultan en un espacio intemporal e internacional.

Sa Fortaleza

Pollença

Built in 1622, this former fortress has a checkered history. The estate was purchased by the Argentine painter, Roberto Ramaugé, in 1919, expanded in the 1920s and 1930s and turned into a hangout for prominent artists. Anglada Camarasa, Tito Cittadini, Roberto Montenegro, Joan Miró, Reynaldo Luza and Pablo Picasso were among the many guests at the time. During the Spanish Civil War, the building was expropriated for military purposes. The property subsequently fell into ruin, and Ramaugé's heirs bought it back in 1982. The new owners renovated the fortress in stages and gradually returned it to its former glory. The building's elegant Mediterranean furnishings and imposing architecture, combined with the property's breathtaking location, have now blended to create a unique and atmospheric whole.

Die ehemalige Festung von 1622 blickt auf eine bewegte Geschichte zurück. Die Anlage wurde 1919 vom argentinischen Maler Roberto Ramaugé erworben, in den 20er- und 30er-Jahren erweitert und zum Treffpunkt einer Künstlerelite. Zu den zahlreichen Gästen gehörten damals u. a. Anglada Camarasa, Tito Cittadini, Roberto Montenegro, Joan Miró, Reynaldo Luza und Pablo Picasso. Nachdem das Gebäude während des Spanischen Bürgerkriegs zu militärischen Zwecken enteignet worden und danach dem Verfall anheimgefallen war, wurde es 1982 von den Erben Ramaugés zurückgekauft. Die neuen Eigentümer sanierten die Festung und die angrenzenden Gebäude schrittweise und führten sie nach und nach in ihre ursprüngliche großartige Form zurück. Der mediterran-elegante Einrichtungsstil, die imposante Architektur und die atemberaubende Lage des Grundstücks verbinden sich nun wieder zu einer einzigartigen atmosphärischen Einheit.

La antigua fortificación de 1622 tiene a sus espaldas una larga y movida historia. En 1919 se hizo con ella el pintor argentino Roberto Ramaugé, quien a lo largo de las dos décadas siguientes fue ampliándola hasta convertirla en punto de encuentro de una élite artística. Entre sus muchos invitados de la época se contaron Anglada Camarasa, Tito Cittadini, Roberto Montenegro, Joan Miró, Reynaldo Luza y Pablo Picasso. Confiscado con fines militares durante la Guerra Civil española, y abandonado después durante muchos años, fue adquirido de nuevo en 1982 por los herederos de Ramaugé. Los nuevos propietarios renovaron progresivamente la fortificación y los edificios colindantes hasta devolverlos a su esplendor original. La decoración, de elegante estilo mediterráneo, se alía hoy con la imponente arquitectura y la privilegiada ubicación del terreno para conformar un conjunto de ambiente inigualable.

Ca'n Suau Vell

Pollença

The owners of this home took the ruins of a traditional finca and turned them into a charming, brightly-colored holiday home, equipped with all the amenities of 21st-century living. Under the aegis of the LF91 architectural firm, they completely transformed the dilapidated building. In the interior, modern furniture creates a successful symbiosis with traditional furnishings and a retro ambience. The original arches and paving stones were integrated into the entrance hall to reflect the farmhouse's history. Natural stone from Binissalem was used for the remaining floors. With its characteristic gray tones, this stone harmonizes perfectly with the modern elements and lends the overall home a slightly rustic feeling.

Hier wurde eine typische verfallene Finca in ein bunt-charmantes Feriendomizil verwandelt und mit den Annehmlichkeiten des 21. Jahrhunderts ausgestattet. Unter der Ägide des Architektenbüros LF91 gelang es, die Ruine komplett zu transformieren. Im Interieur gehen moderne Möbel mit traditionellen Einrichtungselementen und einem Retro-Touch eine gelungene Symbiose ein. Als Referenz an die Geschichte des Gebäudes wurden die Originalbögen und ursprünglichen Pflastersteine in die Eingangshalle integriert. Für die übrigen Böden verwendete man Naturstein aus Binissalem, der mit seiner charakteristischen Grautönung perfekt zu den modernen Elementen passt und dem Gesamtbild etwas Rustikales verleiht.

Se trata en este caso de una ruinosa finca típica transformada en encantadora residencia veraniega y dotada con todas las comodidades del siglo XXI. El despacho de arquitectos LF91 ha sabido transformar por completo aquellas ruinas. En el interior, muebles modernos y piezas más tradicionales conviven en lograda simbiosis de claras reminiscencias retro. En alusión a los orígenes del edificio, en el vestíbulo se han integrado los arcos y adoquines originales de la propiedad. En los demás suelos se ha utilizado piedra natural de Binissalem, cuya característica tonalidad gris encaja a la perfección con los elementos modernos y aporta un toque rústico al conjunto.

The typical Majorcan ceiling beams were whitewashed to create a shabby chic look, which makes the rooms seem tall and airy. The high ceiling was also used to add another floor for a guest room over the kitchen.

Die typisch mallorquinischen Deckenbalken wurden im „shabby chic look" geweißt, was den Räumen ein Gefühl von Höhe und Luftigkeit verleiht. Die hohe Decke wurde außerdem genutzt, um über der Küche eine weitere Ebene für ein Gästezimmer einzuziehen.

Las típicas vigas mallorquinas han sido encaladas en un estilo shabby chic que subraya la espaciosidad vertical de las habitaciones. La altura de los techos se ha aprovechado también para instalar un dormitorio de invitados sobre la cocina.

Ca'n Suau Vell   213

Casa Bauzà

Pollença

This contemporary interpretation of a country house has modern architecture that stands out impressively against the prominent rocky landscape and the oaks and pines that frame the home. The house was designed for the Bauzà family by the LF91 architectural firm. Its distinctive feature is that it is open to nature on all sides and removes the barriers between the man-made and natural worlds. Doors with built-in venetian blinds that can be individually adjusted and form the facade of the imposing sandstone building offer shade and privacy. The linear interior design with modern designer furniture supports the functional, geometric layout of the interior rooms. The open dining, kitchen and living areas are all located on the same level, the space broken up by well-placed staircases and room definitions. The stairs lead to the master bedroom, which occupies the entire upper floor.

Die moderne Architektur dieser zeitgenössischen Interpretation eines Landhauses hebt sich auf beeindruckende Weise von der prominenten Felslandschaft und den das Gebäude umrahmenden Eichen und Pinien ab. Das Haus wurde von der Architekturfirma LF91 für die Familie Bauzà konzipiert. Es zeichnet sich vor allem dadurch aus, dass es sich zu allen Seiten der Natur öffnet und diese in die Innenraumgestaltung einfließen lässt. Als Licht und Sichtschutz dienen die individuell verstellbaren Persiana-Türen, die dem markanten Gebäude aus Sandstein gleichzeitig sein Gesicht verleihen. Die sachlich-grafische Aufteilung der Innenräume wird durch die geradlinige Einrichtung mit modernen Designmöbeln unterstützt. Die offenen Bereiche zum Essen, Kochen und Wohnen, die sich alle auf einer Ebene befinden, werden durch entsprechend platzierte Raumdefinitionen und eine Treppe unterteilt. Diese führt in das einzige Zimmer der oberen Etage – das Hauptschlafzimmer.

Las modernas líneas de esta interpretación contemporánea de una casa rural destacan de manera muy llamativa sobre el paisaje rocoso y los pinos y encinas que la rodean. La residencia fue encargada por la familia Bauzà al despacho de arquitectos LF91. Se caracteriza principalmente por estar abierta en todos los frentes a la naturaleza, que parece penetrar en los espacios interiores. Las persianas correderas ajustables protegen de la luz y miradas indiscretas, y aportan personalidad al excepcional edificio de arenisca. Las líneas rectas del interiorismo y los modernos muebles de diseño subrayan la distribución gráfica y física del interior. Los espacios comunes (comedor, cocina, salón) se encuentran en una misma planta, delimitados por escalones y elementos de definición del espacio. Una escalera conduce al dormitorio, la única habitación de la planta superior.

Index

Refugi a Orient
Orient
Sagristà Simó Arquitectes (architecture)
www.sagristasimo.com

Son Bielo
Serra de Tramuntana
Private property

Torre del Mar
Lluc Alcari
For rent as vacation residence
torredelmar7@googlemail.com

Son Coll
Port d'es Canonge
Private property

Castell de Bendinat
Bendinat
Private property

Casa Son Vida
Son Vida
Cosmopolitan Estates (real estate)
www.cosmopolitan-estates.com
tecArchitecture (architecture)
www.tecarchitecture.com
Marcel Wanders (interior design)
www.marcelwanders.com

Palacio Feliu
Palma de Mallorca
Rialto Living (interior design)
www.rialtoliving.com

Ca'n Montesión
Palma de Mallorca
Private property

Oratorio de Sant Feliu
Palma de Mallorca
Private property

Palacio blanco-negro
Palma de Mallorca
dai[10] (architecture & interior design)
www.dai10.com

Parlament Apartment
Palma de Mallorca
Rialto Living (interior design)
www.rialtoliving.com

Ca'n Blau
Cala Llombards
For rent as vacation residence
Landmark GmbH (real estate)
www.landmark-fine-travel.de

Finca sa Pedra
Santanyí
Private property

Son Silvestre
Santanyí
Private property

Grimalt Charming
Santanyí
Private property

Natural Conclusion
Santanyí
Private property

Casa Neuendorf
Santanyí
Private property
Claudio Silvestrin, John Pawson (architecture)
www.claudiosilvestrin.com
www.johnpawson.com

Son Almendros
Cas Concos
For rent as vacation residence
office@thomaswegner.com
Thomas Wegner (architecture)

La Ruina
S'Horta
For rent as vacation residence
office@thomaswegner.com
Thomas Wegner (architecture)

Son Llodra
Porto Christo
W.S.W Arquitectura (architecture)
www.wummiwagner.com

Son Moix
Manacor
Private property

Sa Canova
Artà
Private property

Es Puig
Artà
Bastidas Architects (architecture)
www.bastidasarchitects.com

Ses Eres III
Artà
For rent as vacation residence
Landmark GmbH (real estate)
www.landmark-fine-travel.de
Bastidas Architects (architecture)
www.bastidasarchitects.com

Sa Fortaleza
Pollença
Rialto Living (interior design)
www.rialtoliving.com

Ca'n Suau Vell
Pollença
LF91 (real estate & project management)
ww.lf91.com
Mestre Paco (interior design)
www.mestrepaco.com

Casa Bauzà
Pollença
LF91 (real estate & project management)
ww.lf91.com
Miquel Lacomba (architecture)
www.mlacomba.com

Biographies

Christine von Auersperg

Born in the German state of Hesse, Christine von Auersperg lives a cosmopolitan life. She has happily made her home in different parts of the world. After studying art and English in Heidelberg, London and Munich, she worked in television for many years and is active in the Nordoff Robbins Foundation and other charitable organizations. She lives with her family in Majorca, Vienna, Berlin and Munich, where she pursues her passions of writing, photography and interior design. Most of all, she likes to cuddle up with her dogs—and also with her husband and kids, when they let her.

Christine von Auersperg ist in Hessen geborene Kosmopolitin. Wo immer sie auf der Welt war, sie war gerne da. Sie studierte Kunst und Englisch in Heidelberg, London und München, arbeitete jahrelang fürs Fernsehen und engagiert sich für ihre Nordoff-Robbins-Stiftung und weitere wohltätige Einrichtungen. Sie lebt mit ihrer Familie in Mallorca, Wien, Berlin und München, schreibt, fotografiert und dekoriert leidenschaftlich gern. Am liebsten knutscht sie aber ihre Hunde – und wenn sie es zulassen, auch ihren Mann und ihre Kinder.

Christine von Auersperg es una cosmopolita nacida en Hessen que se ha encontrado siempre a gusto en todos los rincones del mundo por los que ha pasado. Estudió arte e inglés en Heidelberg, Londres y Múnich y durante muchos años trabajó para la televisión, al tiempo que colaboraba con la fundación Nordoff-Robbins y otras organizaciones benéficas. Reside junto a su familia en Mallorca, Viena, Berlín y Múnich, entregada a sus pasiones: la escritura, la fotografía y la decoración. Lo que más le gusta, con todo, es besuquear a sus perros y, cuando se dejan, también a su marido y a sus hijos.

Tiny von Wedel

Tiny von Wedel grew up in Hamburg and South Africa and studied communications, German, English and psychology. She has lived and worked in Los Angeles, Marbella, Marrakesh, London and other cities around the world. A model-turned-consultant-turned-film producer-turned-entrepreneur-turned-interior designer-turned-yoga teacher-turned-author, she has made Majorca her primary home since 2001, where she works as a free-lance writer. In addition to book projects, she writes about social issues, travel and pure entertainment. Her first novel, "Für immer bis zum nächsten Mal," was published in 2012.

Tiny von Wedel ist in Hamburg und Südafrika aufgewachsen und hat Kommunikationswissenschaften, Germanistik, Anglistik und Psychologie studiert. Sie hat u. a. in Los Angeles, Marbella, Marrakesch und London gelebt und gearbeitet. Model-turned-Kundenberater-turned-Filmproducer-turned-Unternehmer-turned-Inneneinrichter-turned-Yogalehrer-turned-Autor. Seit 2001 lebt sie hauptsächlich auf Mallorca und arbeitet als freie Autorin. Neben ihren Buchprojekten schreibt sie über Gesellschaftsthemen, Reisen und Irrelevant-Unterhaltsames. Ihr erster Roman „Für immer bis zum nächsten Mal" ist 2012 erschienen.

Tiny von Wedel se crió en Hamburgo y Sudáfrica y cursó estudios de ciencias de la comunicación, filología alemana e inglesa y psicología. La vida y el trabajo la han llevado a residir y trabajar en Los Ángeles, Marbella, Marrakech y Londres, entre otros lugares. Ha sido modelo, asesora artística, productora cinematográfica, empresaria, interiorista, profesora de yoga y ahora escritora. Desde 2001 tiene su residencia principal en Mallorca y se dedica a la escritura. Además de sus libros, escribe también sobre cuestiones de sociedad, viajes y los aspectos más entretenidos e irrelevantes de la vida. Su primera novela *Für immer bis zum nächsten Mal* fue publicada en 2012.

Credits & Imprint

Cover photo by Jörg Tietje
Back cover photo by Michael Pentzien

Contents
p 02 by Andreas von Einsiedel (top),
courtesy of J. Knorr & C. Mayer (middle),
Michael Pentzien (bottom)
p 03 by Jörg Tietje

Introduction
Photos by Michael Pentzien (p 05 & p 09),
Photo by Jörg Tietje (p 06)

Refugi a Orient
Photos by Mauritio Fuertes

Son Bielo
Photos by Roman Kuhn

Torre del Mar
Photos by Roman Kuhn

Son Coll
Photos by Roman Kuhn

Castell de Bendinat
Courtesy of Antonio Obrador &
Denario Diseño Integral

Casa Son Vida
Courtesy of J. Knorr & C. Mayer
(p 48, 54, 56-57)
Courtesy of Marcel Wanders Studio
(p 49, 52 bottom, 53, 55 top & middle)
Gaelle Le Boulicaut
(p 50-51, 52 top, 55 bottom)

Palacio Feliu
Photos by Michael Pentzien

Ca'n Montesión
Photos by Uschi Burger-Precht
www.burger-precht.com

Oratorio de Sant Feliu
Photos by Uschi Burger-Precht
www.burger-precht.com

Palacio blanco-negro
Photos by Mauritio Fuertes

Parlament Apartment
Photos by Michael Pentzien

Ca'n Blau
Photos by Jörg Tietje

Finca sa Pedra
Photos by Adriano Bacchella

Son Silvestre
Photos by Michael Pentzien

Grimalt Charming
Photos by Andreas von Einsiedel

Natural Conclusion
Photos by Andreas von Einsiedel

Casa Neuendorf
Photos by Michael Pentzien

Son Almendros
Photos by Lisbeth Hjort

La Ruina
Photos by Lisbeth Hjort

Son Llodra
Photos by Carsten Brügmann

Son Moix
Photos by Roman Kuhn

Sa Canova
Photos by Michael Pentzien

Es Puig
Photos by Bea Krauss
www.beakrauss.com

Ses Eres III
Photos by Jörg Tietje

Sa Fortaleza
Photos by Michael Pentzien

Ca'n Suau Vell
Photos by Mauritio Fuertes

Casa Bauzà
Photos by Mauritio Fuertes

Biographies
p 223 by Bruno Hausch (top),
Gabo (bottom)

Editor	Christine von Auersperg
Texts	Tiny von Wedel
Copy Editing	Ronit Jariv, derschönstesatz, Köln
Editorial Management	Nadine Weinhold
	Regine Freyberg
	Michelle Galindo
Project Coordination	Arndt Jasper
Art Direction	Sophie Franke
Layout & Prepress	Juliane Schröder
Imaging	Tridix, Berlin
Translations	WeSwitch Languages
English	Heidi Holzer
	Romina Russo Lais
Spanish	Pablo Álvarez Ellacuria
	Romina Russo Lais

Published by teNeues Publishing Group
teNeues Verlag GmbH + Co. KG
Am Selder 37, 47906 Kempen, Germany
Phone: +49 (0)2152 916 0, Fax: +49 (0)2152 916 11
e-mail: books@teneues.de
Press department: Andrea Rehn
Phone: +49 (0)2152 916 202
e-mail: arehn@teneues.de
teNeues Digital Media GmbH
Kohlfurter Straße 41-43, 10999 Berlin, Germany
Phone: +49 (0)30 700 77 65 0
teNeues Publishing Company
7 West 18th Street, New York, NY 10011, USA
Phone: +1 212 627 9090, Fax: +1 212 627 9511
teNeues Publishing UK Ltd.
21 Marlowe Court, Lymer Avenue, London SE19 1LP, UK
Phone: +44 (0)20 8670 7522, Fax: +44 (0)20 8670 7523
teNeues France S.A.R.L.
39, rue des Billets, 18250 Henrichemont, France
Phone: +33 (0)2 4826 9348, Fax: +33 (0)1 7072 3482

www.teneues.com
© 2013 teNeues Verlag GmbH + Co. KG, Kempen

ISBN: 978-3-8327-9698-3
Library of Congress Control Number: 2013930378

Printed in Czech Republic.

Picture and text rights reserved for all countries.
No part of this publication may be reproduced
in any manner whatsoever. All rights reserved.
While we strive for utmost precision in every detail,
we cannot be held responsible for any inaccuracies,
neither for any subsequent loss or damage arising.
Bibliographic information published by
the Deutsche Nationalbibliothek.
The Deutsche Nationalbibliothek lists this publication
in the Deutsche Nationalbibliografie; detailed bibliographic
data are available in the Internet at http://dnb.d-nb.de.